EARLY YEARS ACTIVITY CHEST

Early writing

British Library Cataloguing-in-Publication Data
A catalogue record for this book is available from the British Library.

ISBN 0 439 01732 7

ACKNOWLEDGEMENTS
The publishers gratefully acknowledge permission to reproduce the following copyright material:

Irene Yates for 'Invitation kite' © 2001, Irene Yates, previously unpublished.

Every effort has been made to trace copyright holders and the publishers apologize for any inadvertent omissions.

AUTHOR
Jenni Tavener

EDITOR
Clare Miller

ASSISTANT EDITOR
Saveria Mezzana

SERIES DESIGNER
Lynne Joesbury

DESIGNER
Clare Brewer

ILLUSTRATIONS
Andy Cooke

COVER PHOTOGRAPH
Fiona Pragoff

Text © 2001 Jenni Tavener
© 2001 Scholastic Ltd
Designed using Adobe Pagemaker
Published by Scholastic Ltd, Villiers House,
Clarendon Avenue, Leamington Spa, Warwickshire CV32 5PR

Visit our website at www.scholastic.co.uk

1 2 3 4 5 6 7 8 9 0   1 2 3 4 5 6 7 8 9 0

CONTENTS

CONTENTS

Introduction

This Early Years Activity Chest book focuses on early writing and aims to provide educators and carers of children, aged between three and five years old, with a range of practical activities and supporting photocopiable sheets to help teach early writing skills.

The activities within this book provide a scope of ideas to involve the children in a variety of experiences which encourage and develop pre-writing and writing skills. Ideas include using writing patterns to decorate fabric; compiling a feely alphabet frieze; making and writing message cards, invitations and booklets; writing simple signs and clues for a treasure hunt, obstacle course and action game; and using pre-writing skills to help create colourful mobiles and displays.

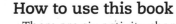

How to use this book

There are six activity chapters, each covering one of the six areas of the Early Learning Goals (QCA). Each activity chapter includes eight activities which follow the same format, with the following sections: 'Learning objective', 'Group size', 'Timing' (this offers a guide which can be adapted according to the particular needs of the children), 'What you need', 'Preparation' (where appropriate) and 'What to do'.

The two sections 'Support' and 'Extension', at the end of each activity, give practical suggestions for adapting or extending the main activity to suit younger or less able children, and older or more able children respectively.

The 'Home links' section offers initiatives to help establish a sound link between the home and the school or nursery. Multicultural links are also suggested when relevant, to help the children gain or maintain an awareness of other countries and cultures, festivals and traditions.

Using the photocopiable pages

There are 24 photocopiable pages in this book, which aim to support or extend individual activities. The photocopiables use a variety of approaches to stimulate the children's interest in learning to write, for example creating a fold-up letter, decorating a flower garden, making an 'I can...' booklet and painting number shapes. A story and a poem are written specially for two of the activities, 'Invitation kite' on page 57 and 'Five speckled eggs' on page 58. Many of the photocopiable sheets can also be used as 'stand alone' activity sheets, to help develop or reinforce particular skills:

- hand/pencil control: 'Jack's beanstalk' on page 62; 'Toy match' on page 70; 'Up and away' on page 72; 'A melting lolly' on page 74; 'Brushes' on page 76
- pre-writing skills: 'Party cake' on page 60; 'Colourful house' on page 63; 'Flower garden' on page 73; 'New bear, old bear' on page 75
- number writing skills: 'Ladybird counting' on page 67; 'Butterfly counting' on page 68; 'Number shapes' on page 69; 'A nest of eggs' on page 71
- correct letter formation: 'Letter formation guides' on pages 77 to 80
- independent writing: 'Animal faces' on page 59; 'I can...' on page 61; 'Mr Crocodile' on page 64; 'Fold-up letter' on page 65; 'Colourful teddy' on page 66.

Using resources

Children enjoy the challenge of using different resources, and by providing a variety of writing tools you can help to stimulate their interest and enthusiasm during pre-writing and writing activities.

The resources mentioned in this book are all usually available in any early years environment, or can be easily obtained. Resources used for activities in this book include colourful felt-tipped pens, thick and thin pencils, giant markers, finger-paints, glitter pens, chalks, paints and brushes in various thicknesses, oil pastels, crayons, fabric pens and fabric crayons.

The resources you provide for the children to write on can also be presented in a variety of inspiring ways, for example, paper and card can be different colours, shapes, sizes and thicknesses, and they can be folded, rolled, cut or even twisted! There is a vast range of exciting pre-writing and writing possibilities, such as creating simple diaries, giant speech bubbles, kites, message flaps, mobiles, tickets, posters, celebration cards, letters and envelopes, labels and signs, streamers and displays, all of

EARLY YEARS ACTIVITY CHEST Early writing

which can be found in the activity chapters of this book.

Links with home

Initiating and maintaining a link between home and your group is very important. A successful link will enable you to establish ongoing co-operation and understanding between all parties: parents, carers, school or nursery staff and the children. If possible, invite parents, carers and grandparents in on a regular basis, so they can keep in touch with their child's world at your group.

Encourage the children to show their parents or carers the displays, mobiles, models and so on that are exhibited around the building. Invite them to sit with their children in the book corner to share the variety of books available, such as commercial books, child-made books, big books, topic books and so on.

You may send home small activities for the children to complete with their parents or carers. Most of the photocopiable sheets within this book, for example, could be used as 'home link sheets' to help reinforce work you have introduced.

If possible, take photographs of the children while they work and play, and display these for parents, carers and children to see.

Opportunities to write

A wide range of ongoing, informal activities can be used to promote an interest in early writing, for example, by setting up imaginative play situations, a card-making centre, a writing corner, a museum/exhibition area and a label tray.

Imaginative play situations – organize an area in the room where the children will be encouraged to write during imaginative play. This area could be transformed, for example, into a café, a doctor's surgery, a shoe shop or a bakery. Provide a variety of resources (such as a small blackboard and chalk, pens, pencils, notepads, an inkpad and stamps, rough paper, old forms and so on) to encourage the children to pretend to write messages, notes, appointments, receipts, cheques, bills and menus.

Card-making centre – set up a small area in the room where the children can use a range of tools and equipment to design and write cards to give to friends and family. These can include invitations and cards with a range of messages. Resources should include a variety of pre-folded cards in different sizes, shapes and colours, pens, pencils, relevant word labels to copy or trace (for example, 'Dear', 'Love from', 'Happy', 'Easter', 'Mother's day' and so on), scissors, glue stick, paper, and collage materials such as ribbon, lace, tissue paper, colourful magazine pictures and envelopes.

Letter-writing corner – provide an area in the room where the children can write, or pretend to write, letters to each other or to take home. Include a 'post-box' in the area made by the children, and boxes or trays containing paper, envelopes, used or pretend stamps, pens and pencils. Display some examples of envelopes clearly labelled with real or imaginary names and addresses so that the children become familiar with the way envelopes are labelled, for example:

Mr Bear
The House
The Road
Big Town
Toyland

Provide each child with a card showing their own name and address to copy or trace.

Labelling – gather together a range of resources to encourage the children to write labels or captions to use around the room. Resources could include short and long strips of paper or card, thick and thin pens, rulers, pencils, sticky tape and Blu-Tack. Invite the children to write or copy name labels to go next to their coat peg, on their drawer, or on a welcome board. Invite older children to write short sentences or captions to accompany their paintings, pictures, photographs or collages.

Museum/Exhibition area – create a special area where the children are invited to display objects, artefacts, pictures and books relating to the chosen topic or theme. Clearly label the exhibits and invite the children to trace or copy these labels. Extend the activity by inviting older or more able children to write some or all of the labels using emergent or 'have-a-go' writing. Encourage the children to update their labels when new items are added to the museum/exhibition area.

If children are provided with a variety of exciting and relevant ways to practise and consolidate their writing skills, they will not only be inspired to develop their abilities, but will also realize the value of writing in everyday communication.

CHAPTER 1

The activities in this chapter encourage teamwork and reinforce self-esteem. There are opportunities for children to role-play everyday situations based around writing, to work together to create an enormous cake decorated in repeated patterns, and to write about things that they can do.

Personal, social and emotional development

GROUP SIZE
Individuals, small or large groups.

TIMING
Ten to 20 minutes.

HOME LINKS
Encourage the children to take a sheet of paper home to write about something they did during the weekend. Add this to their diary when they return to your group. Ask parents and carers to help their children keep a diary during one week of their holiday.

DAILY DIARY

Learning objectives
To reflect on recent experiences; to be motivated to write.

What you need
Writing-paper (A5); coloured paper (A4); pens; pencils; glue stick; hole punch; ribbon; blank labels (20cm x 10cm).

What to do
Provide each child with a sheet of paper and invite them to practise 'have-a-go' writing, describing something they have seen or done during the day. Invite each child to stick their completed writing onto a sheet of coloured paper. Help them to write a label stating the appropriate day and glue it across the top of the page.

Repeat this process on each day the children attend your group. At the end of the week, ask them to help you secure all the sheets belonging to each child together, using a hole punch and ribbon.

Invite the children to design a front cover for their diary and to think of a title, such as 'A week in the life of…' or 'What I did this week, by…'.

Support
Encourage younger children to draw pictures to describe something they have seen or done during the day. This will help to develop their pencil control and will provide pre-writing practice.

Extension
Encourage older children to write their diary and labels on a computer and print them out.

WRITING FOR FUN

Learning objective

To encourage emergent writing during imaginative play situations.

What you need

Table; chairs; paper (lined, coloured, plain, squared); folded card; envelopes; notepads; scraps of paper; felt-tipped pens; crayons; pencils; sharpeners; rubbers; rulers; glue sticks; sticky tape; sticky labels; used stamps; scissors; pen pots; in/out trays; rubbish bin; whiteboard; pinboard; flip chart; toy telephone; calculator; colourful posters; simple dressing-up items; leaflets; brochures.

Preparation

Set up a role-play area which focuses on writing. The many possibilities include a post office, a reception desk for a doctors' surgery, a dentists' practice, a vets' practice or a hotel, a travel agent, a bank, a ticket office for a railway or bus station, and so on. Provide a stimulating environment for the role-play, for example, put up posters and signs to indicate the setting, provide simple dressing-up articles such as hats, name badges, play spectacles and so on, and display relevant brochures or information leaflets.

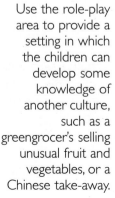

What to do

Invite the children to use the role-play area to act out different roles and scenarios. Encourage them to use emergent or 'have-a-go' writing to create messages, bills, receipts, appointments, dates, letters, prices, and names and addresses using the wide variety of writing equipment provided.

Support

Introduce emergent writing to younger children by encouraging them to use the role-play area with older children.

Extension

Provide old address or telephone books with the letters of the alphabet on each page. Invite the children to use the books during role-play to help them record real or imaginary names under the correct initial letters.

GROUP SIZE
Small or large groups.

TIMING
15 to 30 minutes.

POST-BOX

Learning objective
To work as part of a team to write, post and deliver messages to each other.

What you need
Thick red card; black card; parcel tape; scissors; pens; different-coloured pencils; paper; envelopes; cards; used stamps; postcards; old celebration cards; post person's hat; blue jacket; a name label for each child; bag (or covered box).

Preparation
Invite the children to help create a post-box by bending thick, red card into a tube, and securing it with strong tape. An adult should cut a slit towards the top, so the children can 'post' their 'letters'. Invite the children to help add a red top and black base using thin card or paper, and secure in place using strong tape.

Invite the children to write a simple timetable to glue onto the front of the post-box, giving collection times.

What to do
Place the name labels in a bag or covered box, so they cannot be seen. Invite the children to take it in turns to remove one label. (If the label gives the child's own name, return it to the box and have another go.) Encourage the children to write a letter, card or message to the person on their label. Suggest that they decorate their writing with colourful pictures. Invite the children to place their letter into an envelope, stick the name label and a 'stamp' onto the front, and post their envelopes into the post-box.

Invite the children to take it in turns to dress up as a post person and to collect one letter from the post-box. Help them to read the label and to deliver the envelope to the correct child. Make sure each child receives a message.

Support
Help younger children to write a clear message by copying or tracing your writing. Alternatively, scribe the words beneath a message written using emergent writing. Help each child to read their message when it has been delivered.

Extension
Encourage the children to write, post, collect and deliver several letters to one another.

HOME LINKS
Invite the children to use your post-box to post party invitations, cards and other messages written at home. Take the children to a local post-box or post office to post a letter to someone who lives at their home address.

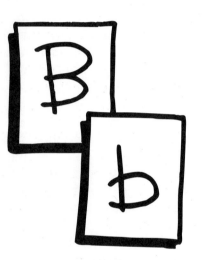

MATCH IT!

Learning objectives
To develop letter recognition and writing skills; to encourage concentration
and observation.

What you need
Card (A5 or A4); thick black pens.

Preparation
Prepare for this activity by inviting each child to help write, trace or copy
the initial letter of their name onto two pieces of card, one in lower case,
the other in upper case.

What to do
Ask the children to sit in a circle, each holding the sheet of card showing
their initial letter in upper case. Place the matching cards showing the
letters in lower case, face down on the floor, in the centre of the circle.
    Invite the children to take it in turns to sit in the centre of the circle
and to select one card. Help them to say the sound of the letter. They
should then find the matching card held by one of the children in the
circle. When the correct card has been identified, they should hand it to
the appropriate child in the circle, and then return to their seat. The
process is repeated until everyone has had a go, and there are no cards
left on the floor.

Support
Provide visual help by displaying an alphabet frieze showing the letters
in upper and lower case.

Extension
Match words or names instead of letters.

SPEECH BUBBLES

Learning objectives

To reinforce writing for a purpose; to gain confidence in speaking in a familiar group.

What you need

An enlarged copy of the photocopiable sheet on page 59 for each child; felt-tipped pens; card; mounting paper; a display board at the children's height; adhesive; a copy of 'Old Macdonald Had a Farm'.

Preparation

Cut out 16 speech bubbles from sheets of card.

What to do

Sing 'Old Macdonald Had a Farm' with the children and encourage them to think about animal sounds. Invite them to cut out and colour in the four animal faces on the enlarged photocopiable sheet. Provide each child with four giant 'speech bubbles', and ask them to think of the noise that each animal makes.

Encourage the children to say and write the sounds on their speech bubbles. Explain that they are writing how noises *sound*, and so they can choose their own way of spelling each onomatopoeia.

When they have completed their writing, mount a selection of the animal pictures and the corresponding speech bubbles onto a display board. Invite the children to think of a title for their display, such as 'What a noise!', or 'Noisy animals'.

GROUP SIZE
Four children.

TIMING
Ten to 20 minutes.

HOME LINKS
Encourage parents and carers to take their children to visit a local farm and observe the animals – what they look like, what sounds they make, and so on.

MULTICULTURAL LINKS
Invite parents, grandparents and carers who have lived in other cultures to share with the children an animal song or rhyme which is traditional to their native country.

Support

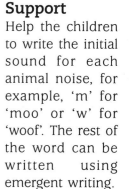

Help the children to write the initial sound for each animal noise, for example, 'm' for 'moo' or 'w' for 'woof'. The rest of the word can be written using emergent writing.

Extension

Invite the children to think about sounding out and writing 'blends', such as 'gr' for 'growl', 'tw' for 'tweet' or 'ch' for 'cheep'. The rest of the word can be formed using 'have-a-go' spelling.

THE ENORMOUS BIRTHDAY CAKE

Learning objective
To inspire teamwork and pre-writing skills.

What you need
Strips of paper in pastel shades (70cm x 20cm); white paint; paintbrushes; narrow strips of colourful crêpe paper; balloons; strips of white card (20cm x 5cm); red tissue paper; a display board at the children's height; black backing paper; a copy of the photocopiable sheet on page 60 for each child.

Preparation
Encourage the children to practise copying some simple writing patterns using the photocopiable sheet.

HOME LINKS
Invite the children to complete one of the writing practice photocopiable sheets at home, for example, 'Colourful house' on page 63 or 'New bear, old bear' on page 75.

What to do
Invite each child to select a strip of pastel-coloured paper. Provide them with white paint and invite them to re-create one of the 'Party cake' writing patterns on the photocopiable sheet along the strip of paper using large, bold brush strokes.

When dry, mount the strips of paper in layers onto a display board covered in black backing paper. You will obtain an enormous cake! Invite the children to help decorate around the cake with strips of twisted crêpe paper and balloons (blown up by an adult).

Invite the children to add strips of white card to the top of the cake to represent candles. Design flames by adding small twists of red tissue paper to the top of the 'candles'.

MULTICULTURAL LINKS
The 'Enormous cake' display does not have to be a birthday cake. It could be a cake to celebrate any religious festival relevant to the children in your group.

Support
Draw simple writing patterns in pencil along the strips of paper for the children to follow using the white paint.

Extension
Invite older or more able children to paint more complicated writing patterns such as repeated letters.

GROUP SIZE
Four children.

TIMING
Ten to 20 minutes.

WHO'S HIDING?

Learning objectives
To reinforce writing and drawing skills; to work successfully as a team.

What you need
A photograph of each child; felt-tipped pens; pencils; four sheets of thin A4 card; glue stick; stapler; A5 paper.

Preparation
Ask parents and carers to provide a recent photograph of their child, or take photographs of the children yourself in advance.

What to do
Provide each child with a sheet of thin A4 size card. Encourage them to use felt-tipped pens or pencils to draw a picture of a door, perhaps their front door, their bedroom door or an imaginary door. When the children have finished the drawing, invite them to stick their photograph onto the reverse side.

Give each child a sheet of A5 paper and ask them to write their name, age and something special about themselves. For example, something they are good at, a game they like to play or something they like to wear. Help each child to stick this piece of writing next to their photograph. Staple all four doors together. Look through the book with the children saying the rhyme:

'Knock, knock. Who can it be?
Let's open the door.
Now who can we see?'

Support
Help younger children to write their name and age clearly. Ask them to tell you their individual special qualities and to draw a picture instead of writing.

Extension
Encourage older children to add as many details as they can to their description. Children that finish quickly can go on to make additional pages about their pets, friends or family.

HOME LINKS
Invite each child to bring in four photographs of family or friends to create a personalized 'Who's hiding?' book. Ask parents to help their children practise writing their name.

MULTICULTURAL LINKS
Provide pictures of homes in other countries to help the children develop some knowledge of everyday life in different cultures.

GROUP SIZE
Individuals, small or large groups.

TIMING
Ten to 20 minutes.

I CAN, YOU CAN

Learning objective
To gain confidence and self-esteem.

What you need
A copy of the photocopiable sheet on page 61 for each child; pens; pencils; stapler; coloured A4 paper.

What to do
Provide each child with a copy of the photocopiable sheet. Encourage them to follow the dotted lines using a pencil to form the words 'I can'. Invite them to draw two pictures about something they can do. Help them to write one word under their picture to describe what they can do, for example, 'dance', 'sing', 'smile' or 'dress'.

When complete, help the children to cut out the sheet and to fold it in half with the writing pages facing inwards. Provide a sheet of folded, coloured A4 paper to use as a cover. Invite the children to decorate the front of their cover and to add a title. Encourage them to write their name on the first page inside their booklet. Display the booklets in the book corner or on a display board at the children's height, along with paintings, photographs and drawings of the children showing what they can do.

Support
Enlarge the photocopiable sheet and help the children to form each letter.

HOME LINKS
Suggest that the children draw a picture at home showing something they can do with their family. Encourage the children to bring parents and carers in to look at their 'I can…' booklets.

Extension
Invite older children to make up a booklet using several 'I can…' pages, or to write short sentences about what they can do on additional blank pages.

CHAPTER 2

Communication, language and literacy

The ideas in this chapter will help children to gain confidence in reading and writing for different purposes. Activities include writing the names of family and friends next to their drawings, writing an invitation that includes specified details, and making an alphabetically ordered reference source of regularly used words.

GROUP SIZE
Individuals or small groups.

TIMING
Ten to 20 minutes.

HOME LINKS
Invite parents and carers to your setting to read other traditional fairy stories to the children. Ask the children to bring in their favourite story-book from home, to share with the rest of the group.

JACK AND THE GIANT

Learning objectives
To hold a pen or pencil effectively to practise following straight lines; to show an understanding of the main elements of a story.

What you need
Enlarged copies of the photocopiable sheet on page 62; scissors; strips of card (50cm x 10cm); small rectangles of card (7cm x 4cm); green wool; sticky tape; paper clips; green felt-tipped pens.

What to do
Provide each child with an enlarged copy of the photocopiable sheet. Ask them to follow the dotted lines using a green felt-tipped pen. Help them to trace, copy or write the words 'up' in the box at the top of the beanstalk, and 'down' in the box at the bottom of the beanstalk.

Invite the children to cut along the thick black lines and to glue their 'beanstalk' onto a strip of card. Ask them to draw a picture of 'Jack' onto one small rectangle of card, and the 'Giant' on a second small rectangle of card. Help them to tape a paper clip onto the back of each picture (see left).

Thread Jack and the Giant onto a length of green wool and secure the two ends of the wool to the top and bottom of the beanstalk. Now, the children can move the pictures of 'Jack' and the 'Giant' up and down the 'beanstalk' as they retell the popular story!

Support
Provide pencils for younger children. Show them how to hold their pencil correctly while they follow the dotted lines.

Extension
Invite older children to write their own version of 'Jack and the Beanstalk', or to write about their favourite character in the story.

THE DARK, DARK HOUSE

Learning objective
To read and write familiar names independently.

What you need
A4 sheets of white card and black paper; pens; pencils; white crayon (or pencil); scissors; glue stick; string; child-safe hole punch; small pieces of fabric (or patterned wallpaper); *Funnybones* by Janet and Allan Ahlberg (Puffin Books).

Preparation
Read the story *Funnybones*. It is about some comical skeletons that live in a 'dark, dark house'.

What to do
Provide each child with a sheet of white card and a sheet of black paper. Help the children to place the black sheet on top of the white sheet, and to glue the sheets together along the left-hand edge. Invite them to trim off the top two corners, to create a house shape, and to punch a hole through the top of the white card using a hole punch.

Ask the children to cut a small shape from fabric (or wallpaper) to represent a lampshade. Provide sticky tape for the children to attach a short length of string to the back of their lampshades. Help them to thread the string through the hole in the white page, and to secure it at the back with tape, leaving the lampshade to dangle freely. Invite the children to use a white crayon (or pencil) to draw a front door, windows and a roof on the black page to represent a 'dark, dark house', and to use bright colours to draw their friends, family or pets on the white page, 'inside' their house. Explain that although the house appears dark and gloomy from the outside, the 'inside' is lit up for a party. Help the children to write the name of each person or pet next to the drawings in their house.

Support
Help younger children to write just one or two main names, for example, 'Mummy', 'Grandad', or their own name.

Extension
Invite older children to write a short sentence next to each person or pet, for example, 'This is Sam', 'Daddy is here' or 'Look at Jojo'.

GROUP SIZE
Small groups.

TIMING
Ten minutes.

HOME LINKS
Provide parents and carers with copies of the photocopiable sheets on pages 77 to 80 so that they can help their children to write letters correctly at home. Alternatively, create your own 'Letter formation guide' according to the particular requirements of your group.

MULTICULTURAL LINKS
Explain that although the Letter Crocodile is a friendly-looking character, real crocodiles can be dangerous. Talk about the variety of animals which live in the wild in Britain and in other countries. If possible, visit a safari park to find out about animals from other parts of the world.

LETTER CROCODILE

Learning objective
To develop skills in letter formation.

What you need
An enlarged copy of the photocopiable sheet on page 64; paint (or crayons); scissors; glue stick; paper fastener; A3 card; display board; sheets of paper (6cm to 10cm square); writing pens; Blu-Tack.

What to do
Provide the group of children with an enlarged copy of the photocopiable sheet. Invite them to paint or colour in the crocodile on the sheet. Help them to cut out the crocodile and his jaw by following the lines on the sheet. Help the children to glue the jaw onto card. An adult should then pin the crocodile's jaw in place using a paper fastener. Mount Mr Crocodile on a display board within easy reach of the children.

Provide the children with an oval cut from a sheet of A3 card to represent a plate. Ask them to glue the 'plate' next to Mr Crocodile's mouth on the display board.

Give each child several sheets of square paper. Encourage them to write a single letter onto each sheet. Let them Blu-Tack their letters onto Mr Crocodile's plate. Pretend with the children that Mr Crocodile enjoys eating a different plate of letters every day! Remove the letters at the end of each day, so that you can repeat the activity the following day using a new set of letters.

Support
Help younger children, individually, to form their letters correctly.

Extension
Invite older children to write short words on separate sheets of paper to place on Mr Crocodile's plate. Use a new set of words each day.

GROUP SIZE
Small groups.

TIMING
Ten to 20 minutes.

HOME LINKS
Ask parents and carers if they would be willing to contribute food for the 'toys' tea party', and invite them.

MULTICULTURAL LINKS
The party invitation, decorations and food could be used to widen the children's awareness of celebrations from different cultures. In December, for example, the party could reflect Hanukkah or Christmas; in January, Eid-ul-Fitr; in September Rosh Hashanah, or Ethiopian New Year, celebrated by Rastafarians.

COME TO MY TEA PARTY!

Learning objective
To write for a purpose, including specified details.

What you need
A copy of the story on the photocopiable sheet page 57; A4 kite-shaped paper; pencils; pens; narrow strips of coloured paper (3cm x 40cm); coloured tissue paper; sticky tape.

What to do
Read the story on the photocopiable sheet to the children. Discuss the story, emphasizing the way the characters sent their invitation on a kite. Provide each child with a sheet of kite-shaped paper, and encourage them to use emergent writing to write an invitation on their kite, asking their favourite toy or teddy to come to a 'toys' tea party'.

Help the children to tape a narrow strip of coloured paper to the base of their finished kite invitation to represent a 'tail'. Provide the children with small rectangles of tissue paper. Show them how to twist the tissue paper to form bows.

Let the children tape several bows to the tail of their kite. Hang the kites to create colourful mobiles, and to reflect what happened in the story 'Invitation kite'. Follow up the activity by suggesting that the children bring in their favourite toy or teddy for a 'toys' tea party' with real (or pretend) food.

To Ted Please come to my party from Tim

Support
Help younger children to write a very simple invitation, for example, just including who it is 'from' and 'to'.

Extension
Encourage older children to add more details in their invitation, such as the date, time and place of the party, and what the guest could bring.

GROUP SIZE
Individuals or small groups.

TIMING
15 minutes.

A LETTER HOME

Learning objective
To gain confidence in writing for an audience.

What you need
A copy of the photocopiable sheet on page 65 for each child; pens; pencils; glue stick; postage stamps.

What to do
Invite each child to write a letter to someone at home, on a copy of the photocopiable page. Encourage the children to use the writing method most suited to their individual ability: emergent writing, copying or tracing. Invite each child to decorate their letter with a colourful border. Help them to cut around the black line on their photocopiable sheet and to fold and seal the page where indicated, so that the writing is on the inside of the folded sheet.

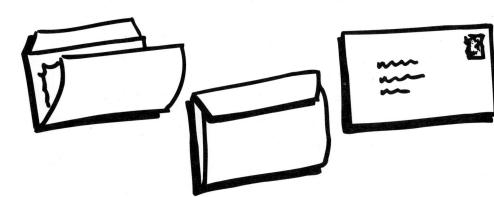

HOME LINKS
Ask parents and carers to help their child write and post a letter to someone at the group.

MULTICULTURAL LINKS
Ask the children to bring in stamps from postcards received from abroad, and use these as a focus for discussion on different countries.

Help each child to write their address on the front of their folded letter, scribing the details for them to copy where necessary, and invite them to place a stamp in the correct position. If possible, organize a walk to a local post-box or post office so that the children can post their own letters.

Support
Help younger children to write who their letter is to and from. Let them draw a picture or pattern in the space in between. Write the address for them.

Extension
Provide older children with a dictionary, and help them to look up how to spell new or difficult words.

GROUP SIZE
Individuals or small groups.

TIMING
Ten minutes.

COLOURFUL TEDDIES

Learning objective
To reinforce writing letters and numbers.

What you need
Photocopiable sheet on page 66; coloured pens and pencils; an alphabet frieze; a number line; real teddy bears; pictures; posters; teddy puppets; samples of toy fabric; a selection of teddy story-books such as *Can't You Sleep, Little Bear?* by Martin Waddell (Walker Books) and *Home Before Dark* by Ian Beck (Scholastic Children's Books).

What to do
Provide each child with a copy of the photocopiable sheet. Invite them to use coloured pens and pencils to decorate the bear with a variety of numbers and letters. Display an alphabet frieze and a number line nearby as visual aids. Help the children to cut out their completed bears. Follow up the activity by helping the children to arrange an interactive teddy bear display.

Support
Enlarge the photocopiable sheet and provide finger-paints. Encourage the children to write the letters and numbers using their index finger.

Extension
Help older children to fill the space on their 'Colourful teddy' photocopiable sheet by writing colour words using the matching coloured pen or pencil.

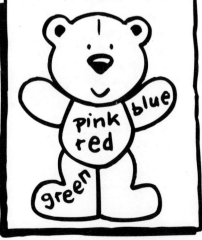

HOME LINKS
Invite the children to bring in items from home to include in your teddy bear display. Invite grandparents in to show or talk about their favourite toys from the past.

AN ALPHABET TRAIN

Learning objectives
To gain awareness of the alphabet; to become familiar with regularly used words.

What you need
Coloured A4 card; 26 A5 envelopes; display board or wall space; 26 sheets of white paper (slightly smaller than A5); thick black pen; strips of white card (15cm x 6cm); glue stick.

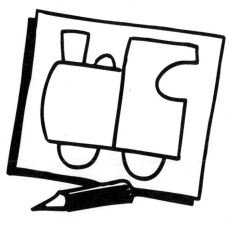

Preparation
Cut out a simple train engine shape from coloured card. Trim the top off 26 sealed envelopes and display them with the engine to represent trucks. Make sure the train is within easy reach of the children.

What to do
Encourage the children to help label the 26 sheets of white paper with the letters of the alphabet, by writing one letter on each sheet using a thick black pen. Help the children to glue the labels on the 26 trucks in alphabetical order.

Invite each child to write their name on a strip of white card. Encourage the children to place their name card in the 'truck' displaying the matching initial letter. Follow up this activity by encouraging the children to write useful or frequently used words on strips of card to add to your alphabet train.

Support
Help younger children to trace or copy their name card.

Extension
Encourage older children to use the alphabet train as a spelling reference during their daily writing activities.

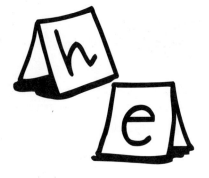

LETTER-FLAP MESSAGES

Learning objective
To link sounds to letters, naming and sounding the letters of different words.

Preparation
Invite each group to think of a simple message to welcome visitors, for example, 'Hello!', 'Welcome!', 'Have fun!', 'Be happy!', 'Good day!'.

What you need
Rectangles of card (40cm x 20cm); pencil; thick marking pens; old catalogues/comics/magazines; glue; aprons; child-safe scissors; the photocopiable sheet on page 80.

What to do
Fold each rectangle of card in half to create a flap. Pencil each letter of the chosen message onto the front of each flap. Provide each child with one or more flaps. Say the letter sounds and show them how the letters are formed. Encourage them to practise following the pencil lines in the correct direction using their finger. When they are familiar with the letter, invite them to write over the pencil lines using a thick marking pen. Ask each child to cut out a picture from an old comic, magazine or catalogue which shows an object or character which begins with the same letter as the one written on their flap. For example, if the message says 'Hello!', the first letter-flap 'h' could have a picture of a house or a horse. For the second letter, 'e', the picture could be an egg or an elephant, and so on for the whole word. Help each child to stick their pictures inside the appropriate flaps.

Hang the flaps in order along the wall or display board, at the children's own height. Use the messages as an interactive display to inspire reading and writing skills.

Support
Help the children to complete a letter-writing practice sheet, such as the photocopiable sheet on page 80.

Extension
Invite older children to draw their own pictures to match the letters of their chosen word.

CHAPTER 3

These imaginative activities will help children with forming and recognizing numerals, and will encourage them to use mathematical vocabulary. You will make number mobiles with number cards and beads, play a number lotto game, and use positional vocabulary to describe a row of flower shapes.

Mathematical development

COUNTING LITTLE BOOK

Learning objectives
To reinforce writing numbers 1 to 5; to inspire saying and using numbers during everyday activities.

What you need
Sheets of green paper (A6 size); red finger-paint; aprons; facilities to wash hands; fine black felt-tipped pens; stapler (for adult use); copies of the photocopiable sheet on page 67.

Preparation
Cut out simple leaf shapes from the green paper to provide five leaves for each child.

What to do
Provide each child with five sheets of leaf-shaped paper. Help them to write 1 on the first sheet, 2 on the second, and so on up to 5. Provide red finger-paint, and invite the children to make one thumb-print on sheet 1, two prints on sheet 2, and so on. When the paint is dry, provide each child with a black felt-tipped pen, and encourage them to use their imagination to turn the red prints into tiny ladybirds by drawing details such as head, legs, spots and antennae on each one.

When complete, staple the five pages together to create a 'counting little book' for each child. Encourage the children to use their book as an ongoing resource to help them write their numbers correctly during everyday maths activities and imaginative play situations.

Support
Provide the children with the photocopiable page sheet on page 67 to help reinforce number writing skills, 1 to 5.

Extension
Invite older children to write the number word on each leaf or help them to make a 1 to 10 counting book.

GROUP SIZE
Small groups.

TIMING
Ten to 15 minutes.

HOME LINKS
Ask parents and carers to count beads, buttons and cotton reels at home with the children, and, if possible, to donate these for the activity.

NUMBER DANGLES

Learning objective
To develop number recognition and number writing skills.

What you need
Enlarged copies of the photocopiable sheet on page 69 for each child; paints; painting equipment (or finger-paints); facilities to wash hands; aprons; card; hole punch; ribbon; wool; colourful beads (or buttons).

What to do
Invite the children to paint or finger-paint each number shape on their photocopiable sheet by starting at the dot and following in the direction of the arrow. When the paint is dry, help the children to cut along the lines to produce nine separate number cards, 1 to 9.

Invite the children to stick each painted number onto a separate sheet of card. For each sheet, help the children to punch one hole in the top and one hole in the bottom, and to tie a length of wool through the hole in the bottom. Then, encourage each child to thread one colourful bead (or button) on the length of wool attached to card number 1, two beads (or buttons) on the wool attached to card number 2, and so on up to number 9.

When the beads (or buttons) are in place, help each child to thread a ribbon through the hole at the top of all nine cards. Hang the ribbons along a display board, across a window or across a corner of the room to produce an unusual set of number mobiles.

Support
Use large, chunky beads, or coloured cotton reels, as these are easier for younger children to handle.

Extension
Invite older children to paint number cards up to 12 (or more).

GROUP SIZE
Pairs of children.

TIMING
Five to ten minutes.

ALL ABOARD!

Learning objective
To recognize and write numerals 1 to 6.

What you need
For the train: five shoeboxes; poster paint; painting equipment; aprons; stapler and hole punch (for adult use); masking tape; thick black felt-tipped pen; string. For the train driver: hat. For the guard: shoulder bag; blank tickets (card or paper 3cm x 5cm); green flag. For the passengers: six small toy characters.

Preparation
Slot two of the shoeboxes together, having removed their lids. Secure them together using string, staples and masking tape, to produce a sturdy engine shape. Invite the children to paint the engine.

Remove the lids on the other three shoeboxes. Invite the children to paint a door on both sides of each box, to represent three trucks. Help the children to write bold numbers: 1 and 2 on the first truck, 3 and 4 on the second truck, and 5 and 6 on the third truck. Join the engine and the three trucks together using a hole punch and string. Add a long length of string on the engine for the children to use to pull the train along the floor.

What to do
Invite the children to role-play train station activities. Choose one pair of children to start the role-play. Encourage the driver to wear a hat and pull the train, and the guard to carry a bag containing blank tickets and a pen. Ask the guard to place up to six toys in the trucks, and to write a ticket showing the correct number for each toy. For example, if four toys have been placed in the trucks beside the numbers 1, 2, 3 and 6, then the guard should write four tickets numbered 1, 2, 3 and 6. The guard should give the tickets to the correct toys, and wave his flag. The driver can then pull the train on a short journey across the room.

Each child taking it in turn to be the driver and the guard, repeat the activity until everyone has had a go in both roles.

Support
Encourage younger children to write the numbers on their tickets correctly by copying the numbers on the sides of the trucks.

Extension
Using a clock with a second hand, challenge the guard to write all the tickets in a given time, for example, in one minute. Ask the driver to watch the clock, and to tell the guard when to start and stop writing.

HOME LINKS
Invite the children to bring in the toy passengers from home. Provide the children with the photocopiable sheet on page 70 to practise hand/pencil control with parents or carers at home.

GROUP SIZE
Small groups.

TIMING
15 to 20 minutes.

HOME LINKS
Ask parents and carers to play counting games with food items at home, such as counting eggs in and out of their egg-box, or counting how many crisp packets there are in a multipack.

MULTICULTURAL LINKS
Introduce the children to traditional rhymes and songs from other countries. *The Singing Sack* compiled by Helen East (A & C Black) includes music and lyrics with background information on songs from around the world.

CRACKING EGGS!

Learning objectives

To encourage counting and writing numbers 0 to 5; to begin to relate subtraction to 'taking away'; to relate numerals to amounts of objects.

What you need

An enlarged copy of the photocopiable sheet on page 58; a copy for each child of the photocopiable sheet on page 71; basket; Plasticine; coloured pens; scissors; glue stick.

Preparation

Invite the children to make five egg shapes from Plasticine. Place the Plasticine eggs in a basket.

What to do

Hold a basket containing five Plasticine eggs, to represent a nest of eggs. Display the enlarged photocopiable sheet on page 58 and say or sing the rhyme 'Five Speckled Eggs' with the children. Invite one of the children to remove one egg at a time from the basket as you say each verse of the rhyme. Continue until there are no eggs left in the basket.

Provide each child with a copy of the photocopiable sheet on page 71. Encourage them to count how many eggs there are in each nest and to write the answer on the appropriate nest, and then to colour in the eggs. Finally, help them to cut their sheet down the centre line, and to tape the two halves together to create a mini number frieze showing the numbers 0 to 5.

Support

Provide a number line showing the numbers 0 to 5 to help the younger children write the numbers correctly.

Extension

Invite the older children to extend their mini frieze by drawing five more nests containing six, seven, eight, nine and ten eggs, along a separate strip of paper. Join the sections together to create a 0 to 10 frieze. Encourage the children to say or sing 'Ten Speckled Eggs'.

GROUP SIZE
Small groups.

TIMING
15 to 30 minutes.

BALLOON SHAPES

Learning objective
To recognize, name and recreate simple shapes.

What you need
A copy of the photocopiable sheet on page 72 for each child; paints; painting equipment; A3 painting paper; aprons; coloured pencils.

What to do
Give each child a copy of the photocopiable sheet and a sharp pencil, and encourage them to follow the dotted lines carefully, in the direction of the arrows. When the children have finished drawing, invite them to colour in the shapes and to identify the name of each shape.

Provide each child with paints and a balloon shape cut from A3 painting paper. Invite the children to fill their balloon-shaped page with an assortment of painted shapes. When the balloons are dry, mount them on a display board or hang them up to create colourful mobiles.

Support
Enlarge the photocopiable sheet to A3 size, and encourage younger children to paint over the dotted lines, instead of painting the shapes free-hand.

Extension
Invite older children to paint repeated patterns on their balloon-shaped painting paper.

HOME LINKS
Ask parents and carers to help children find objects in the home that are circles, squares, rectangles, ovals or triangles, and then to make a list of how many they counted of each. The children could then bring the list in to share with the group.

WHAT'S FOR TEA?

Learning objective
To recognize numerals 1 to 6 and write them.

What you need
Blank gameboard for each child – A4 card, divided into six equal sections; blank game cards – A4 card, cut into six equal sections; pens; pencils; sticky labels; a dice.

What to do
Provide each child with a blank gameboard. Encourage them to write the numbers 1 to 6 in any order, in the six sections. Next, provide each child with six blank game cards. Invite them to write the numbers 1 to 6 on each card. Ask the children to turn over their game cards, and to draw one item of food on the blank side of each card. Provide each child with three sticky labels. Invite them to draw a caterpillar or worm on each label. Ask the children to place the labels on any three food pictures, on their game cards.

To play the game, each player of each pair of children should place their gameboard on a table in front of them and lay all 12 game cards on the table, number side up. The players should take it in turns to throw the dice. If, for example, one player throws a 5, he or she must pick up a game card showing a 5 and place it, picture side up, onto space number 5 on their gameboard. If no number 5 game cards are left on the table, or if the player has already filled space number 5 on his or her gameboard, then the dice is passed onto the next player. This process is repeated until both players have covered all the numbers on their gameboards. The children will now have to work out who the winner is!

The winner is the child with the least number of caterpillars on their gameboard. If both players have three caterpillars, they have to play again until there is a winner!

Support
Use a dice showing dots and make gameboards and cards with dots rather than numbers.

Extension
Encourage the older children to write the number words on the gameboard rather than numerals.

GROUP SIZE
Small groups.

TIMING
Ten to 20 minutes.

HOME LINKS
Ask parents and carers to help their children look for repeated patterns around the home on crockery, wallpaper and upholstery, and to help them copy the patterns in a simplified form.

MULTICULTURAL LINKS
Look at patterns on clothes from different cultures, such as Indian saris and Chinese embroidered tunics or dresses.

FLOWER PATTERNS

Learning objectives
To use everyday words to describe position; to use the names of flat shapes.

What you need
Black paper (15cm x 40cm); green crayons or pencils; coloured sticky paper shapes.

What to do
Invite the children to watch, as you show them how to draw a selection of repeated patterns, for example, curves, zigzags or straight lines.

Provide each child with a sheet of black paper and a green crayon or pencil. Encourage them to choose one of the repeated patterns to draw. Remind the children that it does not matter if their patterns do not look perfect. Invite them to stick coloured shapes on the top of each curve of the green line to create a row of imaginary flowers. Display the pictures where they can be seen easily by the children. Use the pictures to encourage the children to use everyday words to describe position, for example, 'The red flower is next to the blue flower', 'The round, yellow flower is at the end', 'The blue, square flower is in the middle'.

Support
Draw the patterns using a white crayon or pencil for the younger children to go over using a green crayon or pencil.

Extension
Invite older children to draw letter patterns instead of simple curvy patterns.

GROUP SIZE
Small or large
groups.

TIMING
Ten to 15 minutes.

HOME LINKS
Ask parents and
carers to help their
children observe
numbers in their
everyday
environment, for
instance, on food
cans, road signs,
door numbers and
so on.

**MULTICULTURAL
LINKS**
Make simple
Japanese 'carp kites'
by decorating fish
shapes with tissue
paper streamers
and attaching them
to bamboo canes
so that children can
'fly' them above
their heads. Discuss
the origins of carp
kites, telling the
children that they
are made to
celebrate
Kodomono-hi
(Japanese
Children's Day).

FISHY FUN!

Learning objectives

To recognize and write numerals 1 to 5; to use mathematical vocabulary in discussion.

What you need

Light blue backing paper; dark blue backing paper; glue stick; pens; paints; paintbrushes; string; silver foil; sticky tape; white and coloured paper; display board.

Preparation

Cover a display board in dark blue backing paper. Use light blue paper to represent the sky and a darker shade of blue to represent the sea. Invite a child to paint a picture of someone in a fishing boat. When the drawing is dry, help the child to cut it out and to glue it onto the backing paper.

Invite another child to help make a small hook shape using scrunched-up silver foil. Help him or her to tape the hook onto a length of string, and to tape the other end of the string to the fishing boat on the display board. Let the hook dangle freely. Cut out five paper fish shapes (approximately 10cm long) for each child.

What to do

Provide each child with five paper fish. Invite the children to write the numbers 1 to 5 on each fish, and to draw the corresponding number of spots on the reverse side. Help the children to glue the tail of each fish onto the display board. When the glue is dry, the children will be able to flap the body of the fish backwards and forwards to reveal the numbers and the spots.

Use the display to inspire an awareness of mathematical language, with prompts such as, 'How many fish show the number 3?', 'Count how many fish there are altogether', 'Find a fish showing the number 5', 'Look for a fish with less than four spots'.

Support

Write the numbers on the fish for the younger children to trace. Show them where to start, and in which direction to move their pen.

Extension

Encourage older children to cut out their own fish shapes from coloured paper, and to write numbers up to 10 without your help.

CHAPTER 4

These activities help children to focus on looking after each other and their environment. The ideas range from thinking about the effect of rubbish on a garden to observing dewy cobwebs and using line effects to recreate them.

Knowledge and understanding of the world

GROUP SIZE
Small groups.

TIMING
15 to 30 minutes.

HOME LINKS
Ask parents and carers to take all opportunities to reinforce the importance of disposing of litter correctly.

GARDEN RUBBISH

Learning objectives
To encourage pre-writing skills; to explore the importance of looking after the environment.

What you need
A3 paper; red and green paints; paintbrushes; aprons; clean rubbish such as clean sweet-wrappers, screwed-up tissue, silver foil, scraps of fabric, biscuit-wrappers, bottle labels and washed bottle tops; adhesive; a copy for each child of the photocopiable sheet on page 73; red and green pencils.

What to do
Encourage the children to follow the flower writing patterns on the photocopiable sheet, using red and green pencils (red for the flowers and green for the stalks and leaves). Provide each child with a sheet of painting paper and invite them to create a flower garden picture. Ask them to use red and green paints to cover the paper in flowers using the writing patterns that they have practised.

When the paintings are dry, invite the children to fold them in half and to tip clean rubbish all over one half and stick it into place. When the pictures are complete, encourage the children to view both halves of their flower garden. Ask questions such as, 'Would rubbish spoil a real garden?', 'What should people do with their rubbish?' and 'What shouldn't they do?'.

Support
Draw the lines, 'v' shapes and circles in pencil on the painting paper for younger children to paint over.

Extension
Invite older children to paint a decorative border around their paper using repeated patterns such as zigzags or curves.

GROUP SIZE
Small groups.

TIMING
Ten to 20 minutes.

RECYCLING

Learning objective
To use writing skills and select appropriate words to write for a practical everyday purpose.

What you need
Large boxes or crates; used or unwanted items for recycling (for example, clean plastic bottles, plastic pots, cardboard tubes and boxes, newspaper, fabric, and so on); scissors; paints; paintbrushes; masking tape; washable PVA adhesive; aprons; display table; decorative drapes; pens; pencils; writing paper; card.

Preparation
Encourage the children to bring in used or unwanted items for recycling. Store the items brought in by the children in large boxes or crates. Drape a display table with decorative cloth.

What to do
Invite the children to select items from the recycling boxes to create 3-D models. Encourage the children to use their imagination to construct and decorate models. They could create characters such as monster machines, strange animals, robots, imaginary flowers or spacecrafts. Alternatively, link the theme of the models to your current topic. Invite the children to place their completed models on the display table.

Provide each child with a sheet of paper and encourage them to write a label about their model for the display, such as 'This is my robot. By Joe.'. Invite the children to use the method of writing which most suits them, for example, emergent writing, tracing, copy-writing, writing using have-a-go spelling, or writing using simple dictionaries. Help the children to stick their completed writing onto a sheet of folded card to stand next to their model.

Support
Provide younger children with simple labels to copy such as 'I am Tom', 'I made this model' or 'A model by Zoe'.

Extension
Encourage older children to include several details on their label, for example, the name of the model, the materials used, how it was made, what it can do, who made it and so on.

HOME LINKS
Invite the children to bring in models made at home to include in the display. Organize an exhibition day when the children can invite their parents and carers in to admire the models.

MELTING LOLLIES

Learning objectives
To look closely at the changes that occur to materials on a hot day; to practise pencil control.

What you need
Copies of the photocopiable sheet on page 74; ice lolly; dish; sunny window sill; coloured pencils; child-safe scissors; card; glue stick; 20cm dowelling rods; a display board and display table; sky-blue backing paper; yellow disc (30cm in diameter); strips of yellow crêpe paper; an assortment of beach holiday items such as buckets, spades, swimwear, beach ball, beach towel, sand moulds, suncream, sun-glasses; a long trough (for example, a flower tub) or several large tubs (for example, ice-cream tubs); sand; sticks or narrow strips of card.

Preparation
Cover a display board in sky-blue backing paper, stick a yellow paper disc in the centre to represent a sun, and attach twists of yellow crêpe paper to represent the sun's rays. Position a display table beneath the sun. Place a trough or several tubs of sand on the table. Surround the trough with various beach holiday items such as buckets and spades.

What to do
Invite the children to place an ice lolly in a dish in a sunny position. Ask the children to return to the dish at regular intervals to observe the lolly melting. Provide each child with a copy of the photocopiable sheet. Encourage them to use coloured pencils to follow the dotted lines in the direction of the arrows. When the children have completed their lolly shapes, help them to cut them out and to tape a stick (or strip of card) onto the back. Encourage the children to place their lollies in the sand trough, on the display table.

Use the display to inspire discussion about the changes that can occur to some things if left in the sun, for example, chocolate and ice-cream will melt, wet fabric will dry, milk can go sour, small puddles dry up, and so on.

Support
Make an enlarged copy of the photocopiable sheet to allow for bold hand strokes.

Extension
Invite older children to place chocolate, ice-cream, milk, a wet costume and water on concrete in the sun on a hot day, and let them observe and record what happens.

TEDDY BEAR, TEDDY BEAR

Learning objectives
To observe similarities and differences; to practise writing patterns.

What you need
The rhyme 'Teddy Bear, Teddy Bear' in *This Little Puffin…* compiled by Elizabeth Matterson (Puffin Books); copies of the photocopiable sheet on page 75; coloured pens or pencils; an assortment of new and old teddy bears; toy blankets.

What to do
Sing the rhyme 'Teddy Bear, Teddy Bear' with the children. Provide each child with a teddy and a toy blanket. Encourage them to use the teddy to mime the actions of the rhyme as they say the words.

Talk with the children about the similarities and differences between the old bears and the new bears, for example, their appearance, colour and condition. Ask the children to think about what might have happened to the bears to change their appearance, for example, have they lost fur because they were hugged so much, or washed a lot, or is it because they were not looked after?

Provide each child with a copy of the photocopiable sheet. Invite the children to identify which bear looks old and which looks new. Then invite them to follow the writing patterns on the sheet.

Use the completed photocopiable sheets to help create a teddy display. Include other relevant items in the display such as old and new bears, observational paintings and drawings by the children, story-books about bears, such as 'Goldilocks and the Three Bears' (Traditional) and *Old Bear* by Jane Hissey (Red Fox).

Support
Provide younger children with an enlarged copy of the photocopiable sheet. Encourage them to practise following the patterns with their fingers, before they use a pencil or crayon.

Extension
Invite older children to practise their pencil control by following each writing pattern on the photocopiable sheet in a continuous flowing rhythm, without taking their pencils off the page.

APRONS

Learning objective
To attempt writing for a decorative purpose.

What you need
A3 painting paper; triangles of fabric (approximately chin-to-shin length on a child); lengths of ribbon; paints; fabric paints; paintbrushes; masking tape; absorbent paper; aprons.

Preparation
Fold each triangle of fabric in half around several sheets of absorbent paper, so that one corner of the triangle meets the centre of the opposite edge. Lay the fabric and paper on a table with the folded point underneath. Secure around all four edges with masking tape to keep the fabric flat and taut.

What to do
Show the children how to form simple writing patterns such as curves and zigzags. Encourage them to practise the patterns on sheets of paper using paints. Then, place each child in front of a piece of fabric secured to the table, and encourage them to repeat their writing patterns on the fabric, using fabric paints. When the patterns are dry, help each child to make a simple apron by inserting a length of ribbon under the fold of their triangle. Use the ribbon as waist ties.

Initiate discussion about when, where and why people need to wear aprons. Invite the children to wear their aprons during everyday activities such as gluing or painting. Encourage them to think about other forms of protective clothing such as firefighters' outfits, painters' overalls, divers' wetsuits and so on.

Support
Encourage younger children to paint random patterns on the aprons, for example, circles, lines and crosses.

Extension
Older children could decorate their aprons with their own name or a chosen word, perhaps using a different colour for each letter.

CLEAN AND HEALTHY

Learning objectives
To find out about daily health routines; to use a pencil effectively.

What you need
Copies of the photocopiable sheet on page 76; pens and pencils; a collection of real brushes used for keeping clean and healthy (such as nail brushes, hairbrushes, toothbrushes, afro combs and so on).

What to do
Encourage the children to complete each dot-to-dot drawing on their sheet, to reveal three different types of brush. Invite the children to colour in the completed outlines.

Show the children a collection of real brushes (include in this collection a nail brush, a hairbrush and a toothbrush). Ask the children to identify the three brushes on their sheet in the collection of real brushes. Talk with the children about why and when each brush is used. Use the activity to inspire discussion about keeping clean and healthy.

Support
Sing the song 'Here We Go Round the Mulberry Bush' with the children. Include verses for cleaning hands, brushing hair and brushing teeth and mime the actions.

Extension
Invite the children to help you make a big book entitled 'This is the way we...', or 'Here we go round the mulberry bush'. Encourage the children to write and draw pictures for each page of the book, to match the verses in the song.

PIP AND SEED CARDS

Learning objectives
To compare a variety of pips and seeds; to write chosen messages.

What you need
A5 coloured card (folded in half); A5 writing paper; pens and pencils; washable PVA adhesive; a variety of dry pips and seeds (such as apple, orange and watermelon pips, and sunflower and nasturtium seeds); small tubs or trays; pictures (or real examples) of the fruit or plant which derives from each seed or pip; apple, knife (adult use) and plate, or a sunflower head containing seeds.

What to do
Show the children the collection of pips, seeds, fruit and flowers (or pictures of fruit and flowers). Explain which plant or fruit matches each pip and seed. Cut open an apple to show the children some pips in their original place, or show them a sunflower head containing seeds.

Provide each child with a sheet of folded card, a tray of pips and seeds and some adhesive. Invite the children to use their imagination to stick the seeds and pips decoratively onto the front of their card. Help them to write a message of their choice to someone special on a sheet of paper to place inside their card.

Encourage each child to use a method of writing to suit their individual need and ability: emergent writing, copy-writing or tracing.

Support
The pips and seeds might be rather awkward for younger children to use, so invite them to create a sprinkle picture. To do this, help them to spread streaks of adhesive randomly over the front of their card, and encourage them to sprinkle the pips and seeds onto the adhesive. Knock off the excess pips and seeds and leave them to dry.

Extension
Invite the children to plant a selection of seeds (nasturtiums are easy to grow), so that they obtain first-hand experience of seeing plants grow from seed.

SPIDER WEBS

Learning objectives
To observe and discuss features of the natural world and the man-made world; to encourage mark-making skills.

What you need
Extra adult help (to supervise children during the walk; magnifying glasses; large paper discs in dark colours (dark green, deep grey, dark brown, black); silver or white finger-paint; tiny discs of shiny foil or silver paper; glue stick; glitter (white or silver); children's torches; washable PVA adhesive.

Preparation
Plan a safe place for the children to walk on a dewy morning, where there will be plenty of cobwebs. Mix a little PVA adhesive in with the finger-paint to make the paint slightly sticky before it dries.

What to do
On a dewy morning, take a small group of children outside to observe cobwebs. Encourage them to use the magnifying glasses to observe the glistering dew drops on the threads of each web, but remind them to be careful not to damage the cobwebs. Invite them to talk about their observations.

Back inside, provide each child with a disc of dark-coloured paper, and some finger-paint. Encourage them to create their own cobweb design on the paper, using the finger-paint to mark out a pattern. While the paint is still wet, help the children sprinkle glitter over their web picture. When this is dry, invite the children to stick small silver discs over their shiny web to represent dew drops.

Display the finished web pictures around the room, on the ceiling and in dark corners. Create an unusual visual effect by turning the lights down and providing the children with torches. Invite them to shine their torches on the webs to make them sparkle. Encourage the children to talk about their observations using descriptive language.

Support
Encourage younger children to paint random lines and patterns on their paper disc, as this still proves very effective when covered in glitter and shiny paper.

Extension
Invite older children to use shiny threads and beads and help them to sew cobweb patterns onto discs of dark fabric.

CHAPTER 5

Physical development

There are lots of opportunities for different kinds of movement with the ideas in this chapter. Children can make writing patterns in time to music, create name cards with bouncy letters to shake, and write directions for an obstacle course, amongst other inspiring activities.

GROUP SIZE
Up to four children.

TIMING
Ten to 20 minutes.

HOME LINKS
Invite parents and carers to use story-books with fairly dense text, and to encourage their children to find specific letters and words on each page.

HIDE-AND-SEEK LETTERS

Learning objectives
To form letters correctly and clearly for use in an action game; to develop an awareness of 'letter sounds'.

What you need
26 card squares; pens; an alphabet frieze; copies of photocopiable sheets on pages 77 to 80 (for 'Support').

What to do
Share the 26 blank cards between the children. Help them to write a different letter on each card using an alphabet frieze as a visual aid. Help the children to form their letters correctly so that all 26 letter cards are clear to read. Ask the children to look away while four of the letter cards are hidden around your setting. Invite the children to help one another to find all four cards. Repeat the game, until the children have collected a complete set of letter cards showing all 26 letters of the alphabet. Help the children to sort the cards into alphabetical order. Encourage them to say the sound of each letter.

Support
Provide younger children with copies of the photocopiable sheets. Help them to write each letter correctly, by following the dotted lines on the sheet.

Extension
Encourage older children to write simple letter blends, for example, 'sh', 'th', 'ch', 'sp', 'st', 'bl', onto squares of card, then play *Hide-and-seek* with these.

GROUP SIZE
Small groups.

TIMING
Five to 15 minutes.

HOME LINKS
Tell parents and carers about your activity, and suggest that they extend the idea at home by encouraging their children to use expressive movements to different types of music.

MULTICULTURAL LINKS
Provide examples of music or songs from different countries or cultures for the children to listen and draw to. The World Music Network (tel: 020-74985252) supply a wide selection of CDs of traditional music from around the world.

MUSICAL MARKINGS

Learning objectives
To listen and respond to music; to use large and small hand and arm movements to create a colourful picture showing an array of random lines and patterns.

What you need
Tape recorder (or CD player); instrumental music (for example, the hymn 'Morning Has Broken', which is slow and gentle, the theme to 'Chitty, Chitty, Bang, Bang', which is fast and strong; or 'We All Live in a Yellow Submarine', which has a combination of gentle and forceful sounds); large sheets of paper; thick crayons.

What to do
Provide each child with a large sheet of paper and a selection of crayons. Invite the children to draw patterns on the paper as they listen to some music. Encourage them to listen carefully to variations within the music, and to respond accordingly. Suggest that they try doing fast hand movements to uptempo music; steady or controlled movements to calm music; short, quick movements to repetitive or 'jerky' beats, and so on, always trying to reflect the feeling of the music in the marks that they make. During the slow, gentle music, the children could draw slowly to create flowing lines, curls and swirls. During strong, forceful music, they might draw zigzags, dots and dashes.

Encourage the children to let their hands move freely across the page in time to the music, until their sheet of paper is full of colourful random lines and patterns, creating an original abstract design.

Support
Introduce the activity to younger children by inviting them to observe a group of older children as they create patterns to music.

Extension
Invite older children to decorate fabric with fabric crayons. Secure the fabric onto the table using masking tape to keep it taut and let the children draw on it. Help them to turn their decorated fabric into cushions for the book corner, bags to store toys, or curtains for the home corner.

GROUP SIZE
Individuals or small groups.

TIMING
Ten to 20 minutes.

BOUNCY LETTERS

Learning objectives
To develop manipulative skills; to encourage letter-writing.

What you need
Coloured pens; glue stick; paper strips (5cm x 15cm); card.

What to do
Provide each child with the same number of paper strips as there are letters in their first name. Help them to fold each strip twice, to produce a zigzag shape with three sections and to write the letters of their name onto the front section. Cut card into strips and help the children to glue their letters onto a piece of card in the correct order.

When the name cards are complete, invite the children to knock or shake them so that the letters bounce. Use the bouncy name cards as unusual labels for the children's artwork. Alternatively, mount all the bouncy name cards together on a board to create an eye-catching 'welcome' display.

Support
Provide younger children with one large, pre-folded strip of paper. Invite them to paint their initial letter on the front and to decorate around their letter with dots, lines or patterns.

Extension
Invite older children to extend this idea by creating gift cards containing 'bouncy-letter' messages or greetings.

HOMELINKS
Ask parents and carers to try a similar idea with their children to create name cards for their bedroom doors.

MULTICULTURAL LINKS
Invite the children to help create a 'welcome' board which displays the word 'welcome' in various foreign languages in bouncy letters.

WHAT'S IN A NAME?

Learning objective
To handle a range of writing tools with increasing control.

What you need
A variety of writing tools, for example, pens, chalk, crayons, paints, pastels, pencils, finger-paint; A4 paper; black card.

What to do
Provide each child with a sheet of paper and a wide range of writing tools. Invite them to experiment with writing their name on the sheet of paper using all the different pens, paints, pastels and so on. Encourage them to write using an assortment of styles, for example, large and small letters, lower- and upper-case letters, letters going across and down the page, thick and thin letters, and so on.

When complete, mount the colourful name posters onto black card and display on the wall under a heading such as 'Name gallery'.

Support
Encourage younger children to use a wide range of writing tools to make a 'poster' displaying random patterns, lines and shapes, or showing the initial letter of their name written in different sizes, colours and styles.

Extension
Invite older children to include their surname on their poster, or to copy a simple rhyme or poem using a different writing tool for each word, line or verse.

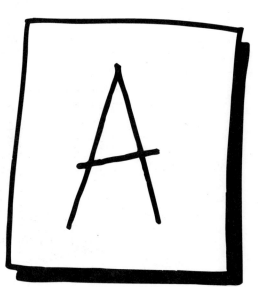

TREASURE HUNT

Learning objective
To write clearly for a purpose.

What you need
Some treasure (any suitable treat or keepsake for each child, for example, some 'well done' stickers, coloured pens or pencils, or seasonal items such as Christmas crackers or small Easter gifts); paper; pens; a 'treasure box' (such as a shoebox with a lid, or a plastic container with a lid); a safe area inside or outside which is spacious and has plenty of places to hide your treasure box; extra adult assistance; three coloured cards labelled 'clue 1', 'clue 2' and 'clue 3'; three pegs (or large paper clips).

What to do
Invite the first group of children to help organize a treasure hunt for the children in Group 2. Ask Group 1 to place the selected treasure into the treasure box, and then to hide the treasure box somewhere within your chosen area, inside or outside.

Walk a little way away from the treasure box, until it is out of view. Then, encourage Group 1 to think of a clue which would help Group 2 to find the box. Note the children's ideas on a piece of paper, and mark the spot with a coloured card saying 'clue 3'. Attach a peg or large paper clip to the card.

Now walk a little further away, until clue 3 is out of view.

Invite Group 1 to think of a clue to help Group 2 find clue 3. As before, note their ideas on paper, and mark this spot with a coloured card saying 'clue 2'. Repeat this process once more and mark the final spot with a card saying 'clue 1'.

Read the three clues to the children in Group 1, for example 'Look in the toy-box', 'Look next to the book box', and 'Look under the dressing-up box'. Ask them to copy, trace or write one clue each. Help the children to peg each clue onto the appropriate coloured card.

Invite the second group of children to begin at the first clue and to follow each clue in order until they find the treasure.

Repeat the activity at a later date, to enable the two groups of children to swap roles.

Support
Help younger children to create clues which are short and simple by using pictures or signs such as arrows to replace words. Begin by organizing treasure hunts with just one or two clues.

Extension
Encourage older children to think of rhyming clues. For example:
'Look behind the tree
And you will see a clue
That has been left by me'.

GROUP SIZE
Small groups.

TIMING
Ten to 15 minutes.

THIS WAY!

Learning objectives
To develop hand control; to communicate using written symbols.

What you need
For the signs: A5 folded card; paper (half A5); glue stick; thick red felt-tipped pens. For the 'obstacle course': a safe, spacious area inside (or outside); equipment suitable for use in an obstacle course (for example, low level benches, hoops, tunnels, soft mats and so on).

Preparation
Invite the children to help set up an obstacle course using objects that they can go under, over, through and around.

What to do
Provide the children with thick red felt-tipped pens and some paper. Encourage them to draw an arrow shape on each sheet of paper using bold lines and 'v' shapes. Help the children to glue each arrow picture onto a sheet of folded card.

Ask the children to stand the arrow signs around the obstacle course pointing in the direction that should be followed. Invite them to use the obstacle course by following the 'signs'. Repeat the activity by encouraging them to change the position of the arrow signs to create a different route around the course.

Support
Mark out each arrow by drawing fine pencil lines or dots for younger children to follow.

HOME LINKS
Ask parents and carers to encourage their children to look out for signs and symbols in their everyday environment, such as road signs and clothes care instructions.

Extension
Encourage older children to write simple instructions instead of arrows, for example 'this way', 'turn left', 'turn right', 'go under', 'climb over' and so on.

MULTICULTURAL LINKS
Explain that the alphabet is like a set of symbols. Show the children examples of writing from different countries that contain letters which do not appear in the English alphabet, for example, Arabic, Hebrew or Japanese writing.

GROUP SIZE
Small or large groups.

TIMING
15 to 30 minutes.

FRUITY LETTERS

Learning objectives
To gain an awareness of the foods which help to keep us healthy; to identify types of fruit.

What you need
Red, yellow, green, orange and purple A4 and A5 paper; bright-coloured felt-tipped pens or paints in the same colours as the paper, plus brown; scissors; display board; black backing paper.

Preparation
Cover a display board with black backing paper. Cut out the shapes of familiar fruit using the appropriate coloured paper, for example, red or green for an apple shape, yellow for a banana.

What to do
Provide each child with a paper fruit shape and a felt-tipped pen or paint in the appropriate colour, ensuring that it

is a darker tone than the one of the paper it will be used on. Bright yellow rarely shows, even on pale yellow paper, so provide light brown pens/paint for yellow fruit and vegetables.

Encourage the children to write the initial letter of the fruit repeatedly all over their paper shape. Repeat the activity letting each child decorate a fruit shape which requires a different initial letter. Invite the children to help arrange the completed paper fruit shapes on the black display board to represent a pile of fruit. Use the display to inspire discussion about foods which help to keep us healthy.

Support
Give younger children individual help in forming their letters correctly.

Extension
Invite older children to write upper- and lower-case letters, or the whole word on each paper shape.

HOME LINKS
Ask parents and carers to help their children to prepare a fruit salad at home, or to provide fruit and equipment for observational drawing.

MULTICULTURAL LINKS
Discuss the origins of fruit from other countries and investigate ways they are grown and harvested.

BEANBAGS, BALLS AND BOXES

Learning objective
To encourage fine and gross motor skills..

What you need
Three large cardboard boxes; beanbags; small soft balls; paints; thick and thin paintbrushes; aprons; facilities to wash hands.

What to do
Provide each pair of children with a cardboard box and paints. Encourage them to use thick and thin paintbrushes to decorate the outside of their cardboard box with writing patterns such as straight and wavy lines, zigzags, curves, dots, dashes, curls and whirls.

When the paint is dry, invite the children to use the three boxes as a resource for throwing and aiming challenges. For example, ask them, 'How many times can you throw a beanbag into the boxes in one minute?', 'How many balls, out of say six, can you land in the boxes?', or 'Who will be first to knock down a stack of three boxes using a beanbag?'.

Support
Introduce younger children to writing patterns using one of the photocopiable sheets, such as 'Up and away', page 72; 'Party cake', page 60; or 'Colourful house', page 63.

Extension
Invite older children to paint a large number inside each box to provide a scoring system.

CHAPTER 6

The ideas in this chapter will inspire children to use writing for creative purposes. The inventive ideas include decorating a 'magic' rug with repeated patterns, creating a 'feely' alphabet, and writing and decorating café name signs for the role-play area.

Creative development

CREATIVE CLOTH

Learning objectives
To use symbols and recognizable letters and numbers to decorate fabric; to explore colour and pattern in design.

What you need
Two pieces of plain fabric cut to exactly the same size (approximately 100cm square); a selection of fabric paints and permanent colour markers; masking tape; sheets of newspaper; needles and thread; cushion stuffing.

Preparation
Lay the pieces of fabric out on a flat surface protected with newspaper, and fasten the edges securely with masking tape.

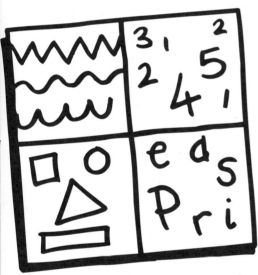

What to do
Divide the first piece of fabric into four equal sections using a ruler and a permanent marker. Invite the children to take it in turns to help fill each section differently, with shapes, numbers, letters and repeated patterns.

When this piece of fabric is complete, ask the children to paint or write their names on the second one. When both pieces of fabric are dry, sew them together along three sides and fill with cushion stuffing before sewing the last side, to make a special cushion for the book corner.

Support
Place an alphabet chart and number line nearby to help the children form their letters and numbers correctly. Provide name cards for individual children to copy.

Extension
Instead of drawing shapes and patterns in two sections, include one section for capital letters and one for rhyming words such as 'cat, mat, hat' or 'dog, fog, log', and so on.

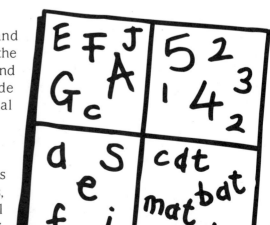

GROUP SIZE
Individuals, or small
or large groups.

TIMING
20 to 30 minutes.

FLYING CARPET

Learning objectives
To develop hand control; to inspire imagination.

What you need
Pieces of card (20cm x 30cm); paints; paintbrushes; aprons; scissors; hessian; patterned rug; teddies or dolls; masking tape; strong fine thread.

Preparation
Cut two strips of hessian for each child (20cm x 5cm).

What to do
Place the rug on the floor and invite the children to sit on it. Inspire their imagination by explaining that the rug is a flying carpet which can take them anywhere they want to go. Discuss with the children where they would like the rug to take them. Invite them to make a flying carpet for their teddy or doll.

Provide each child with a sheet of card and some paints. Encourage them to use their imagination to decorate the card to resemble a patterned rug, using colourful patterns such as loops, circles, curves, lines, hooks and so on.

When the paintings are dry, help the children to tape two strips of hessian onto the reverse side of their card. Assist them in making a fringe along both ends of their card by fraying the overhanging fabric. The card should now resemble a mini rug or flying carpet. Attach thread to each corner of the card for hanging, and invite the children to sit a small teddy or doll onto each 'flying carpet'.

Support
Offer younger children plenty of assistance with attaching the fabric and creating a fringe.

Extension
Encourage older children to plan their design on a separate sheet of paper. Ask them to include patterns which flow across the page, such as zigzags, or to use repeated letter patterns.

HOME LINKS
Encourage parents
and carers to make
up flying carpet
adventure stories
with their children
at home using rugs
as props.

MULTICULTURAL LINKS
Look at pictures or
real examples of
rugs from other
countries, for
example, Persian
rugs, Indian rugs or
Islamic prayer mats.

GROUP SIZE
Small groups.

TIMING
20 to 30 minutes.

HOME LINKS
Encourage parents and carers to take their children to look at real fish at an aquarium, a garden centre or a park.

LETTER FISH

Learning objectives
To explore shape and form in three dimensions; to form recognizable letters.

What you need
A4 paper; A4 card; black crayons; orange and yellow paints; paintbrushes; aprons; glitter; PVA glue; scissors; thread; strips of tissue paper or fabric (50cm x 5cm) in various shades of green; sticky tape.

Preparation
Make several simple fish templates using sheets of A4 card.

What to do
Provide the children with A4 paper and a fish template. Help them to draw a fish shape and cut it out. Encourage each child to mark a head section on their fish using a black crayon, and to fill the body and tail with black letters. Provide an alphabet frieze as a visual aid and help each child to form their letters correctly. Invite the children to paint over their fish shape with orange or yellow paint (the paint will not stick to the wax crayon, so the letters will remain clear). When the paint is dry, encourage them to decorate the back of their fish with glitter, shiny paper, or sequins.

Help each child to loop their fish and attach its head to its tail. Tape thread to the top of each fish and hang them from the ceiling or a display board, along with several narrow strips of green tissue paper or fabric, to create the effect of a shoal of letter fish swimming through seaweed.

Support
Help younger children to draw simple patterns on their fish shape.

Extension
Encourage older children to write relevant words on their fish shapes, such as 'fish', 'splish', 'splash', 'swim' and so on.

PATCHWORK PATTERNS

Learning objectives

To develop pre-writing skills; to create a decorative patchwork design.

What you need

Coloured A4 paper; A1 paper; felt-tipped pens; six strips of card (30cm x 10cm); pencil; ruler; scissors; adhesive; display board; examples of patchwork (or pictures from craft books, catalogues and so on).

Preparation

Cut seven hexagons from sheets of coloured A4 paper so that they are exactly the same size. Use a pencil and ruler to draw two evenly spaced guidelines across each hexagon to divide it into three horizontal sections. Draw a different writing pattern on each strip of card to create six writing pattern sample cards.

What to do

Show the children the examples or pictures of patchwork. Talk about tessellating patterns and look for examples of tessellation in the children's immediate environment, for example, pavements, floor tiles, carpet patterns and so on.

Provide each child with felt-tipped pens and a paper hexagon. Invite them to decorate their paper shape with three different writing patterns in the three sections, using the sample cards as a visual aid.

When the hexagons are complete, help the children to glue the seven decorated shapes onto a large sheet of paper to create a patchwork pattern. Use the pattern as the centrepiece for a display about tessellation and patchwork. Include relevant pictures, books, drawings and fabric examples in the display.

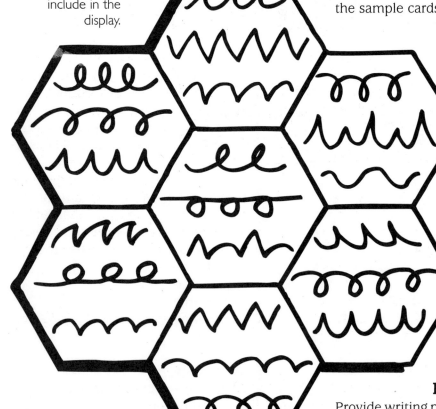

Support

Help younger children to trace the writing patterns. Alternatively, draw a pattern in the top section of their paper shape, then encourage them to copy the pattern in the remaining two sections using two different colours.

Extension

Provide writing pattern samples which are slightly more complicated, such as a series of letter shapes with ascenders and descenders.

SEA SCENE

Learning objectives

To explore colour texture and shape; to form repeated patterns.

What you need

For the background: strips of paper (20cm x 40cm) in various shades of blue, grey and green; paints in shades of blue, grey, blue-green and white; paintbrushes in various thicknesses; aprons; a display board covered with dark backing paper. For the foreground: colourful paper (in various sizes); colourful paints; small printing objects (sponges, cotton reels, old bricks, strips of thick card and so on); blue cotton; sticky tape; glitter glue or glitter and PVA glue mixed together.

What to do

Provide each child with several strips of paper and paints in underwater shades. Encourage the children to observe while you paint some examples of repeated patterns. Invite them to copy the examples or to make up their own patterns to represent waves.

When the paint is dry, pin or staple each strip of paper onto the display board end-to-end in horizontal lines. Make sure each one bends outwards slightly, to provide a 3-D wave-like appearance.

Next, invite the children to use their imagination to paint real or imaginary sea creatures onto colourful sheets of paper. When the drawings are dry, help the children to cut them out. Tape cotton onto the back of each creature and hang amongst the waves on the display board. You could use the fish made in 'Letter fish' (page 51) as an additional decoration.

Support

Provide younger children with large strips of paper to allow for bold hand movements.

Extension

Allow older children a high degree of independence as they hang their own sea creatures amongst the waves on the display board. Encourage them to write relevant captions for the display such as 'Find the octopus', 'How many fish?' or 'Find two starfish'.

FEELY LETTERS

Learning objective
To explore texture and collage to create large letter shapes.

What you need
26 sheets of A5 or A4 card; 26 sheets of black A5 or A4 paper; pencil; scissors; selection of collage materials with different textures (such as wool, tissue paper, sandpaper, clean lolly sticks, buttons, fur fabric, silky fabric, smooth plastic, rough string, cotton wool and so on); adhesive.

Preparation
Draw the outline of each letter of the alphabet in lower case on the 26 sheets of card. Cut out each letter shape.

What to do
Show the whole group of children the 26 letter shapes. Help them to say the sound of each letter. Provide letter shapes for each pair of children and encourage them to select one of the collage materials to glue onto their letter shapes. For example, the 'a' could be covered in silky fabric, the 'b', in snippets of rough string, the 'c' in cotton wool, and so on. Help the children to trim off excess collage fabric from each letter shape so that all the letters are clear to read. Invite each pair of children to glue their letter shapes onto a sheet of black paper. Display around the room at the children's own height to create an unusual textured alphabet frieze.

Support
Guide younger children's hands over each letter shape to help them become familiar with correct letter formation.

Extension
Invite older children to close their eyes while they feel a letter shape. Can they identify the name or sound of the letter shape?

GROUP SIZE
Small groups.

TIMING
15 to 30 minutes.

TWISTED STREAMERS

Learning objectives
To develop hand control; to use their imagination in art and design.

What you need
A piece of A1 paper for each child; colourful paints; paintbrushes; aprons; scissors; masking tape; string; pegs.

What to do
Provide each child with a sheet of A1 paper and some colourful paints. Invite them to cover their paper with colourful stripes. Ask the children to leave a gap, as small as possible, in between each stripe. When the paint is dry, help the children to cut along the gaps, leaving a band of between 10cm and 20cm at one edge of the page, creating a giant fringe effect. Help each child to roll the uncut section on their fringe and to seal the roll with masking tape to create a streamer.

Make an impressive indoor or outdoor display by pegging the streamers to a length of string. Take them down for children to experiment and play with on a windy day.

Support
Paint guidelines on the A1 paper for younger children to paint within.

Extension
Provide a thin paintbrush and encourage older children to paint several rows of repeated handwriting patterns. Invite them to cut between each row to create the streamer effect.

HOME LINKS
Invite parents and carers to play a 'stripe spotting' game when they are out with their children, looking for stripes in an everyday environment, such as the pattern of wooden fences, zebra crossings or clothing.

OUR CAFÉ

Learning objectives

To write and decorate name posters for a café in the structured play area; to encourage emergent writing during role-play activities.

What you need

For the café: two small tables; two chairs; table-cloth; plastic plates; cups; saucers; cutlery; pretend food; small vase of flowers; dressing-up clothes (hat and coat for the customer; apron, notepad and pen for the waiter or waitress); toy till; toy telephone. For the posters: A3 coloured paper; A4 white paper; colourful felt-tipped pens or paints; pencils; crayons; hole punch; ribbon; two cup hooks; a display board (or a spare chair).

Preparation

Invite the children to help you set up a café in the structured play area. Cover a table with a cloth and add some cutlery, pretend food, a vase of flowers and two chairs. On the second table, place a till, a telephone, a notepad and a pen. Place a dressing-up box containing the role-play clothes nearby.

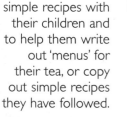

What to do

Provide each child with a sheet of A4 paper and some colourful felt-tipped pens or paints, and invite them to write a large sign for the café, incorporating their own name, for example, 'Emma's Café', 'Peter's Café' and so on. When their sign is complete, help each child to glue it onto a sheet of coloured A3 paper. Encourage them to use their artistic skills to decorate the coloured paper around their sign. Attach a ribbon to the top of each sign using a hole punch. Hang the signs on two cup hooks on the wall near the café, or secure them firmly one at a time with drawing pins.

Invite the children to select a different café name each time they play. Encourage them to use the notepads and pens for emergent writing, for example, taking orders, telephone messages, bills and so on.

Support

Write the café names for younger children to copy.

Extension

Encourage older children to decorate the coloured edge of their poster with relevant words, such as 'Welcome', 'Eat in or take away' or 'Tasty food!'. Invite them to write pretend menus on sheets of folded card.

Invitation kite

Come to Amanda Floppy Doll's party at three o'clock

Amanda Floppy Doll felt quite unhappy. It was her birthday. Tuppy, the Toy Elephant, wanted to have a birthday party for her. But how would they get the rest of the toys to come?

'We can't knock on everyone's door,' Tuppy grumbled. 'They live too far away.'

'We could ask them to pass a message on,' said Amanda.

Tuppy said, 'There's not time. If every toy passed the message on to two more toys it would take...' He curled up his trunk and tried to think. But there were *such* a lot of toys in ToyTown, and he wasn't very good at sums. 'Well,' he said darkly, uncurling his trunk, 'it would take a *long* time.'

Peter Cuddly Rabbit said, 'I've got an idea.'

'*Silly!*' said Amanda Floppy Doll, tossing her head. 'Everybody knows Cuddly Rabbits don't have good ideas.'

'But it *is* a good idea,' said Peter, feeling very hurt.

Tuppy, who couldn't think of a single idea of his own, said, 'He might as well tell it to us. And then if it isn't any good, we needn't take any notice.'

'I *suppose* so,' said Amanda.

Peter Cuddly Rabbit thought Amanda was in such a bad temper he didn't really want to tell his idea anyway. But, on the other hand, he quite fancied the idea of a jolly party and there might be lots of carrots.

He said, 'We could make a kite. We could write an invitation on it and send it sailing off. *Everybody* would see it and come to the party.'

'That *is* a good idea,' said Tuppy Elephant gruffly. He was a bit upset he hadn't thought of it himself.

Amanda Floppy Doll was so delighted that she forgot her bad temper immediately and gave Peter Cuddly Rabbit a big hug. 'You are *so* clever!' she said.

The three toys gathered everything they needed to make the kite. On it they wrote, in huge letters, 'Come to Amanda Floppy Doll's party at three o'clock'.

They went to the Town Square and tied the end of the kite string to the lamppost so that it wouldn't disappear into the sky.

Then they went back home to get the party ready.

At three o'clock, every toy in ToyTown turned up! 'Thanks to Peter Cuddly Rabbit's *good* idea!' said Amanda happily.

© Irene Yates

Five speckled eggs

(To the tune of 'Ten Green Bottles'.)

Five speckled eggs
in a wonky nest.

Five speckled eggs
in a wonky nest.

But if one speckled egg,
should accidentally fall,

'Smash!'

There'll be
four speckled eggs
in a wonky nest...

© Jenni Tavener

Animal faces

Colour in and cut out the faces.

Animal faces

Party cake

Use coloured pens or pencils to follow the patterns.

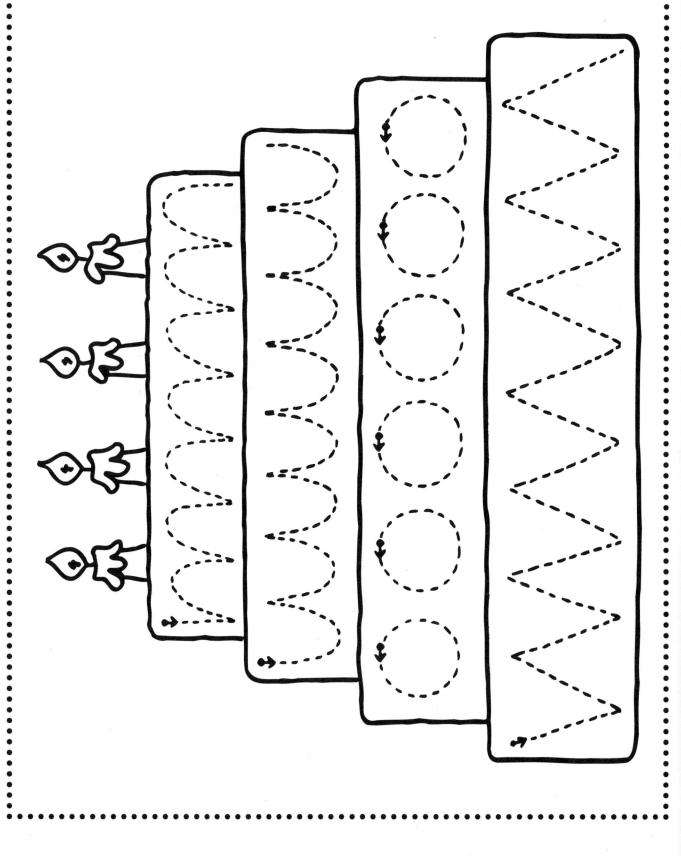

Party cake

I can...

Draw and write about two things that you can do.

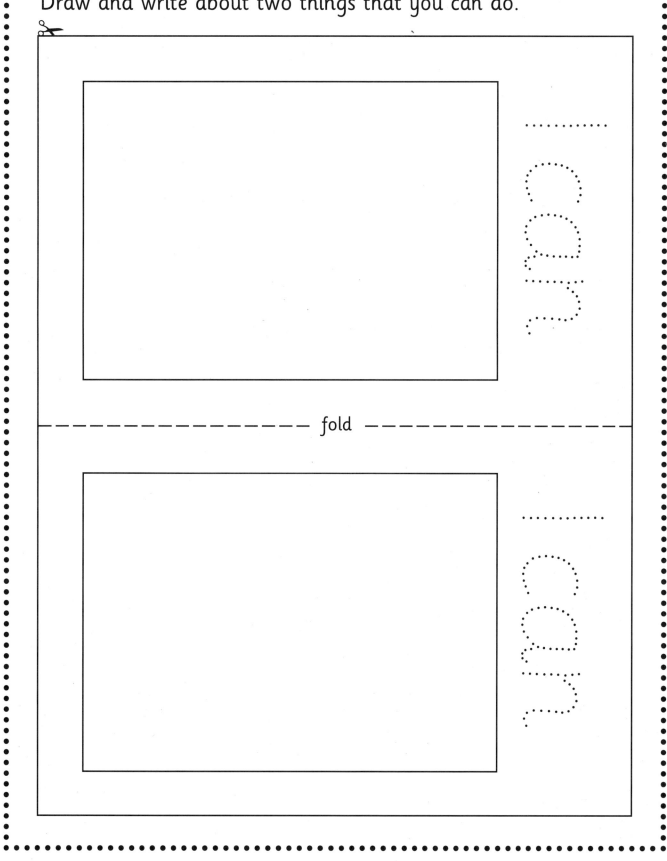

fold

Jack's beanstalk

Use a green pen to follow the dotted lines.
Write the words 'up' and 'down' in the boxes.

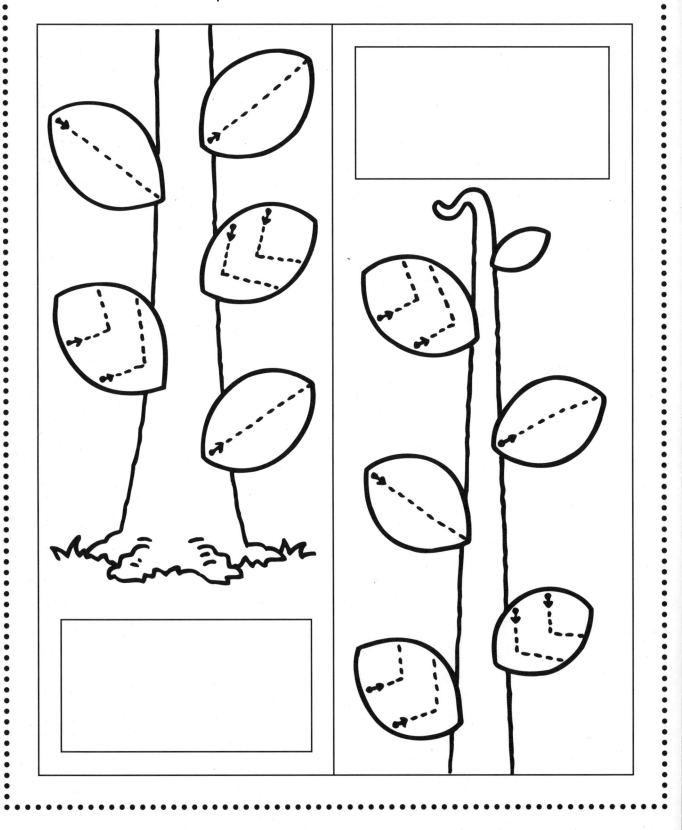

Colourful house

Follow the lines using colourful pens.

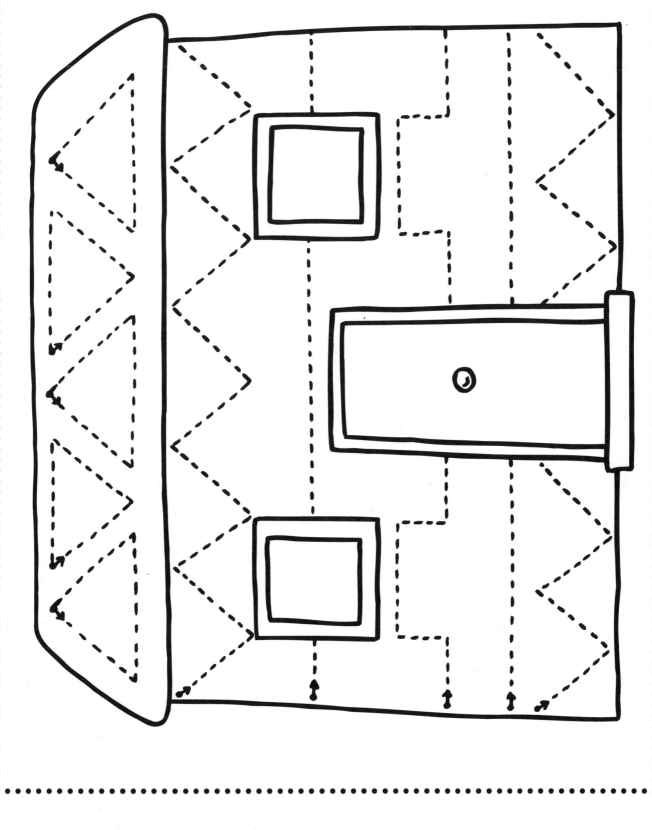

Mr Crocodile

Cut out both shapes. Secure the crocodile's jaw with a paper fastener.

Mr Crocodile

Fold-up letter

Write your message. Cut out, fold, seal, stamp, address and post!

To _____

From _____

Colourful teddy

Fill the teddy with colourful letters.

Ladybird counting

Count the dots on each ladybird. Write the answers in each box.

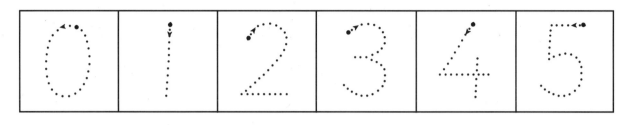

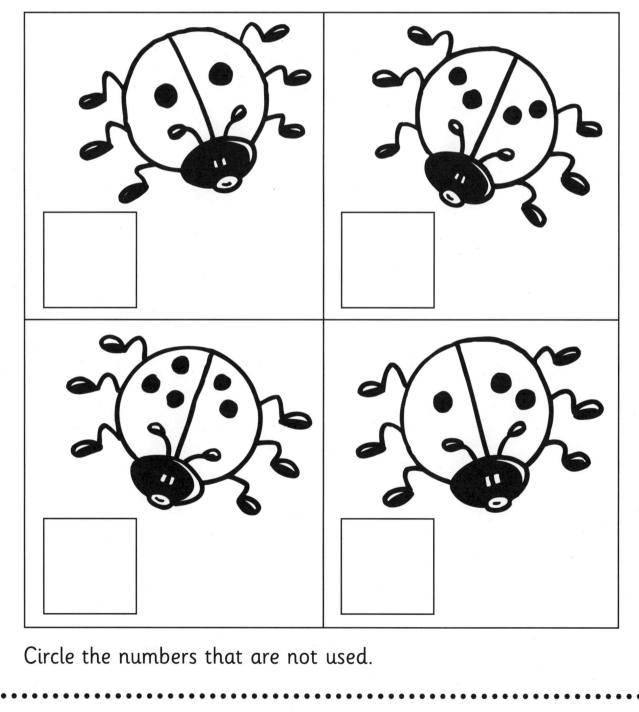

Circle the numbers that are not used.

Butterfly counting

Count how many shapes there are on each butterfly.

Circle the numbers that are not used.

Number shapes

Use paints and a paintbrush, or finger-paint, to write the numbers.

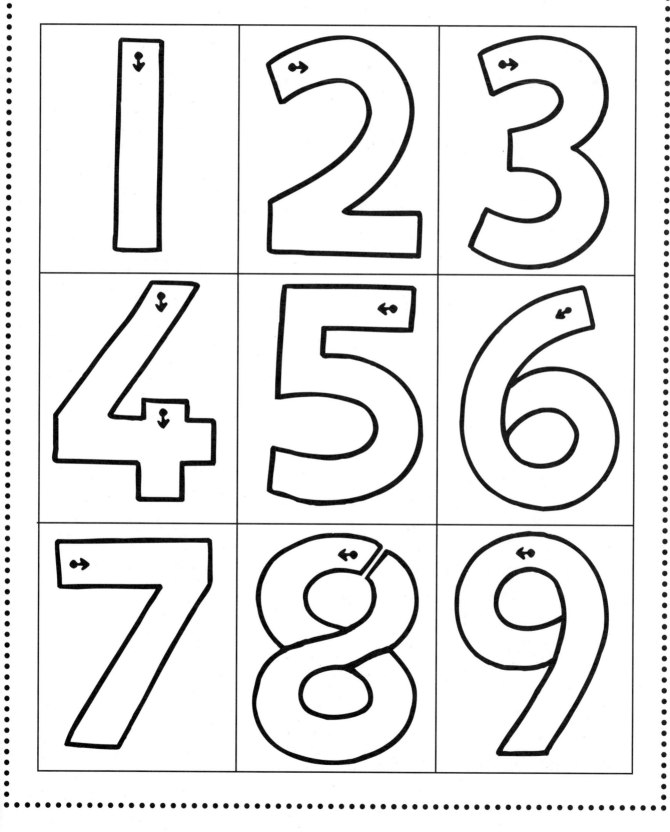

Toy match

Follow the dotted lines to show the engine driver, the guard and the passengers where to sit.

A nest of eggs

Count how many speckled eggs there are in each nest. Write the answers on the nests.

Up and away

Start at the dots and follow the arrows.

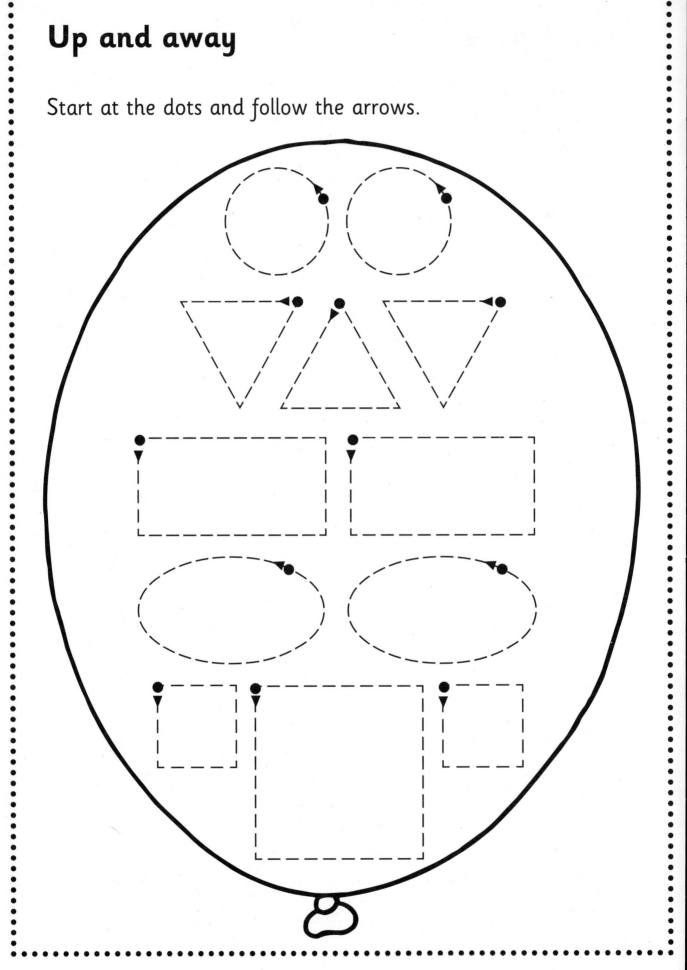

Flower garden

Colour in the flowers using red for the circles and green for the lines and 'v' shapes.

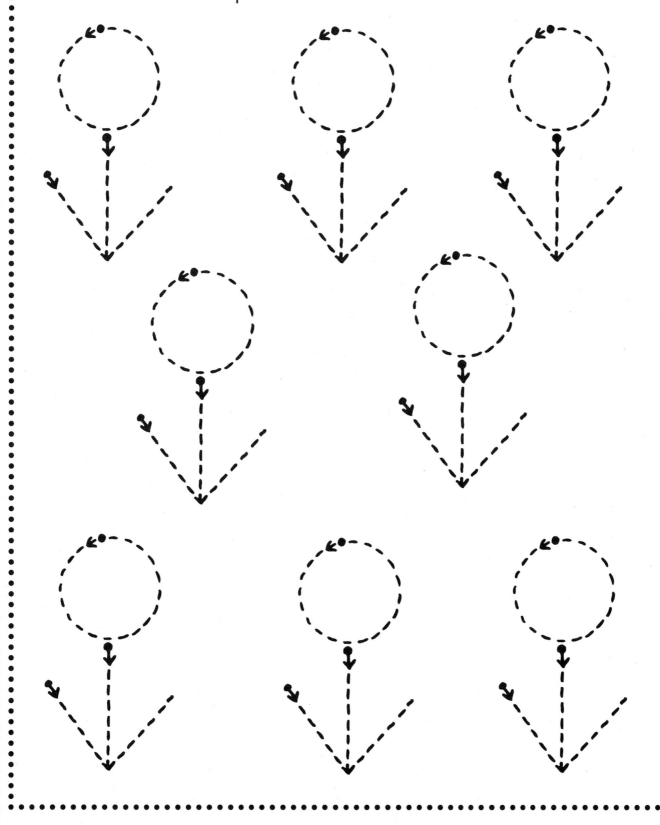

A melting lolly

Start at the dots
and follow the
dotted lines
in the direction
of the arrows.

A melting lolly **EARLY YEARS ACTIVITY CHEST** Early writing

New bear, old bear

Start at the dots and follow the dotted lines in the direction of the arrows.

New bear, old bear

Brushes

Follow the dot-to-dots to reveal the three brushes.

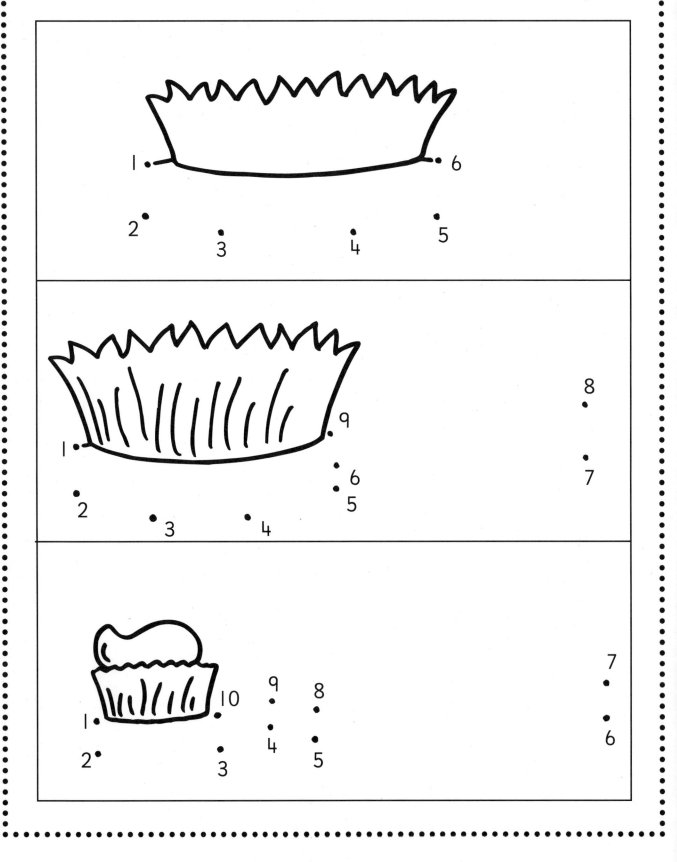

Letter formation guide, a to f.

Start at the dot and write each letter in the direction of the arrow. Say the sound of each letter.

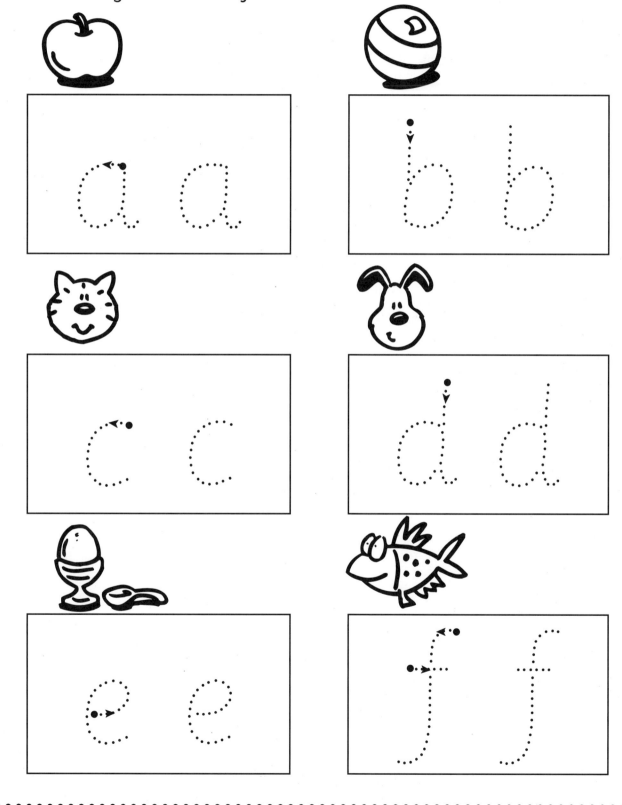

Letter formation guide, g to l.

Start at the dot and write each letter in the direction of the arrow. Say the sound of each letter.

Letter formation guide, m to r.

Start at the dot and write each letter in the direction of the arrow. Say the sound of each letter.

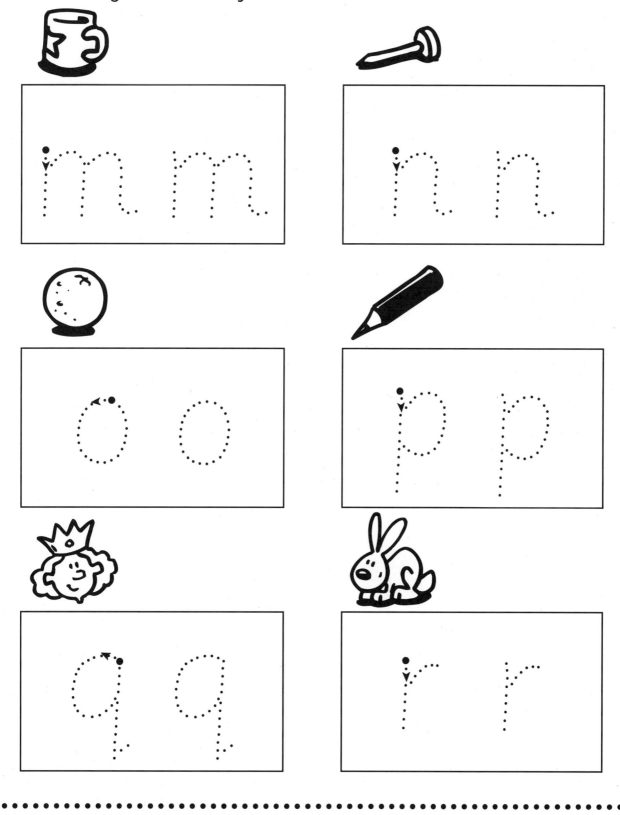

Letter formation guide, s to z.

Start at the dot and write each letter in the direction of the arrow. Say the sound of each letter.